ALL-AMERICAN
FOLK ARTS AND CRAFTS

ALL-AMERICAN
FOLK ARTS AND CRAFTS

WILLIAM C. KETCHUM, JR.

RIZZOLI
NEW YORK

First published in the United States of America in 1986 by
RIZZOLI INTERNATIONAL PUBLICATIONS, INC.
597 Fifth Avenue, New York, NY 10017

Library of Congress Cataloging in Publication Data

Ketchum, William C., 1931–
    All-American folk arts and crafts.

    1. Folk art—United States.   2. Decorative arts—
United States.   I. Title.
NK805.K468   1986   709'.73   86-42739
ISBN 0-8478-0765-7

Created and produced by Cynthia Parzych Publishing, Inc.

Editor: JAY HYAMS
Designer: ANA ROGERS

Composition by Trufont Typographers, Inc.
Separations by Laser Graphics, Hong Kong
Printed and bound by Mandarin Offset Marketing, Ltd., Hong Kong

CONTENTS

PAGE 2: Schoolhouse quilt, pieced cotton with appliqué design; by Pat Karambay, Newington, Connecticut, 1985–86. The traditional schoolhouse pattern is enhanced in this piece by the addition of titles and phrases from American patriotic songs. The creator remarked, "When I was making this piece, it was the first time in a long time that I had thought in depth about my own pride in being an American." OPPOSITE: Whirligig in the form of Abraham Lincoln, carved and painted wood with tin; by Janice Fenimore, Madison, New Jersey, 1978. A traditional whirligig form is here used to honor a great American patriot.

ALL-AMERICAN

FOLK ARTS AND CRAFTS

INTRODUCTION

If the glory of Europe is its fine arts, the products of centuries of academic training and royal patronage, then surely America's glory lies in its folk arts, the products of an equality of opportunity never dreamed of in the mother countries. The creative spirit behind America's folk arts reflects the special nature of American society, a society very different from European society. Even in the early 19th century, Europeans marveled at the absence in America of what they had come to think of as "natural" social distinctions:

"In this country no man calls another master. . . . In mentioning this term 'master,' which is obsolete here, I may remark that I never knew a native American who wore livery; nor would extra wages induce them to put it on. I have frequently made the enquiry, but always found that those in liveries were foreigners. . . . All that takes place in this country is on the principle of an equitable exchange; there is considered to be no obligation on either side." (J. C. Loudon, *Gardener's Magazine*, 1831)

Inherent in this spirit of equality was the idea that art was not the domain of a privileged few—as it was in Europe—but was for all and could be made by all. Americans made portraits, quilts, weathervanes, baskets, and an enormous variety of other art and craft objects with an enthusiasm that was unbounded, even if it wasn't always equalled by aptitude or training. As Francis J. Grund noted:

"As far as I am able to ascertain, there is, in America, no deficiency of talent either for drawing or painting; but there is little or nothing done

Quilt made to memorialize the 1876 centennial, pieced cotton commemorative kerchiefs; United States, ca. 1876. Mass-produced printed textiles could be readily adapted to the needs of the quilter, as in this unusual example.

Train pull toy, turned and painted wood with lithographed paper decoration; R. Bliss Manufacturing Company, Pawtucket, Rhode Island, ca. 1893. This train was among the many toys made to capitalize on interest in the Columbian Exposition of 1893, held in Chicago, Illinois. Lincoln Park was the location of the exposition grounds.

for their encouragement. The education of an American artist with the only exception of a few not very competent drawing masters is altogether left to himself." (Francis J. Grund, *The Americans in Their Moral, Social and Political Relations*, 1837)

What Grund saw as an artistic shortcoming, others saw as an invitation to freedom of expression. Indeed, Americans viewed themselves as born artists—and developed a healthy skepticism toward the work of professional artists. As one German artist complained:

"The Americans in general do not estimate genius. They come to me and ask what I want for my pictures, and I tell them. Then they say, 'How long did it take you to paint it?' I answer, 'so many days.' Well, then they calculate and say, 'If it took you only so many days, you ask so many dollars a day for your work; you ask a great deal too much; you ought to be content with so much per day, and I will give you that.'" (Frederick Marryat, *Diary in America, with Remarks on Its Institutions*, 1839)

It's hardly surprising that those who so valued their freedom would often choose for their subject matter the emblems or symbols of that freedom: the eagle, the flag, the presidents and other statesmen of the nation. Nor is it surprising that these American folk artists also portrayed events, both historic and humble, that signified for them the freedom they cherished.

Thus, Uncle Sam, the goddess of Liberty, George Washington, and other recognized American symbols have been portrayed by generations of American folk artists; the flag, with its ever-growing

number of stars, has been depicted flying over rural scenes and from the masts of Yankee clippers; the eagle has been formed into weathervanes and figureheads. At the same time, it is touching to see the renditions of simple country scenes and vignettes of the home, for these often reflect essential American values, such as prosperity, religious freedom, or the opportunity for education. These observations on American life, created by untrained artists, provide some of the most telling documents of the American experience.

Of course, the results were not always equal to the artist's aspirations. This was true even in the nation's capital, where the desire to honor in art waxed strongest. The *New-York Daily Tribune* of July 23, 1868, described the city of Washington as a "town full of statues, of dwarfs, cripples, rocking horses and drunken Indians. Washington, nearly naked, sits out in the rain colossally, pointing to the Patent Office, where his breeches are. Lincoln is a baseball pitcher on top of a column. A pea-green Jefferson, deaf and dumb, is asking alms, with a paper, before the White House. Near by Gen. Jackson is riding to victory in a landscape of foaming mugs of lager-bier."

Criticism of this sort never deterred the folk artist. Throughout the country, and for over two hundred years, Americans have continued to make their folk offerings to the spirit of America. Women have created quilts to honor the centennial of 1876 and the bicentennial of 1976. Itinerant portraitists have captured the likenesses of the Republic's citizens. Folk painters of widely varying skills have created

Trolley pull toy, turned and painted wood with lithographed paper decoration; R. Bliss Manufacturing Company, Pawtucket, Rhode Island, ca. 1893. This toy horse-drawn trolley was made in imitation of the real trolleys that ran from downtown Chicago along Grand Boulevard to the Jackson Park fair grounds.

scenes depicting the industry, commerce, politics, and agrarian interests of the growing nation. Great events, such as the landing of Columbus in 1492 and the Columbian Exposition of 1892, have inspired the creation of not only art but toys. Ceramics, wood, glass, and metals have all served as material for the creative and the patriotic.

Although folk expression can assume many forms and employ myriad techniques and textures, there is still a tendency to think of the folk artist as "an artist" in the traditional academic sense. How far even the American folk painter was from the rigors of academic training may be gathered from the following case history, the true-life story of a 19th-century folk portraitist told in his own words:

"I put up at a tavern and told a Young Lady if she would wash my shirt, I would draw her likeness. Now then I was to exert my skill in painting. I operated once on her but it looked so like a rech I throwed it away and tried again. The poor Girl sat nipped up so prim and look so smileing it makes me smile when I think of while I was daubing on paint on a piece of paper, it could not be called painting, for it looked more like a strangle cat than it did like her. However, I told her it looked like her and she believed it." (*The Travel Diary of James Guild*, Vermont Historical Society Proceedings, 1937)

Itinerant artists like Guild may have been untutored in the European academic sense, but they were often extremely talented—and they had a very American eye for the main chance. If you didn't need a portrait of the family, the family house, or the family business, perhaps you needed something else in the way of art. The Pennsylvania painter Frederick Kimmelmeyer, for example, advertised his many skills thus: "Signs in the best and most elegant manner . . . Guilds and Reguilds frames for Pictures, Mirrors &c. in a durable and substantial manner." Such artists also offered instruction to "ladies and gentlemen that wish to be taught in the polite art of drawing and painting."

Such "professionals" were a distinct minority. Most of the people who created the folk art that honored our nation did so out of love and with little or no training. Their art came from the heart. As a farm wife who was also a maker of hooked rugs wrote for the *Rural New Yorker* in the late 19th century:

"I enjoy making my own designs. I never knew how to sing or paint or draw; no way to express myself, only by hoeing, washing, ironing, patching, etc., and while I never hope to accomplish anything extraordinary, I do love to plan out and execute these rugs that are a bit of myself, a blind groping after something beautiful."

That the "groping" of this and countless other American folk artists was far from blind but rather the finest expression of the hopes and aspirations of our country is clear from the legacy of patriotic folk art they have left us.

OPPOSITE: **Harvest jug, salt-glazed stoneware with cobalt-blue floral decoration; United States. Made to honor the 1876 centennial, this piece is of a form once used to carry water to thirsty field hands.** ABOVE: **Proprietary medicine bottle, mold-blown glass; made for Wishart's Pine Tree Tar Cordial, Philadelphia, 1859–80. The pine tree embossed on this bottle reflects the importance of that wood in early American history. For over a hundred years, masts of sailing ships were made from the great pines of New England's forests, and Maine adopted the pine as its state tree.**

RIGHT: "Centennial" quilt, cotton with appliqué design; by G. Knappenberger, Pennsylvania, 1876. Quilts were among the many creations inspired by the 1876 centennial. Interestingly enough, although this quilt includes traditional Pennsylvania motifs, such as the heart and bird basket, it lacks patriotic symbols like the eagle and flag. FOLLOWING PAGES: *Champion Quilt*, acrylic on canvas; by Susan Slyman, New York, 1984. Slyman captures the awards ceremony at a state fair, with the proud creator posing beside her prize-winning quilt.

Stars and Stripes Forever

For almost all people in all countries, the national standard has great evocative power, and this nation is no exception. The Stars and Stripes evolved from earlier banners and became official when the Continental Congress, on June 14, 1777, passed a resolution decreeing that "the flag of the United States shall be thirteen stripes, alternate red and white, with a union of thirteen stars of white on a blue field, representing a new constellation."

The emotional attachment of the citizenry to this symbol of their new freedom seems to have been instantaneous, and the original bond has grown only stronger with the passing of time. References to the flag abound in the growing Republic's history; and as the nation grew, so grew the flag. The flag so anxiously watched by Francis Scott Key during the night of September 13–14, 1814—the flag immortalized as "The Star-Spangled Banner"—had fifteen stars and fifteen stripes (the custom of adding both a star and a stripe for each new state to enter the union ended in 1818, by which time there were twenty states, and the flag was becoming unwieldy; Congress voted to use only the original thirteen stripes and to indicate each new state by the addition of a star).

Generations of American schoolchildren have learned the immortal lines offered by a 90-year-old woman in response to a rebel's attempt to tear down the national standard:

"Shoot if you must, this old gray head,

But spare your country's flag, she said."

(John Greenleaf Whittier, "Barbara Frietchie," 1864)

Weathervane in the form of the goddess of Liberty holding the American flag, copper with paint and gilding; attributed to J. W. Fiske or A. B. & W. T. Westervelt, New York City, 1880–95. This noble figure bears the national colors with obvious pride. Weathervanes were sometimes made in the form of the flag itself, as its broad surface readily caught even the most subtle breeze, but few such vanes have survived.

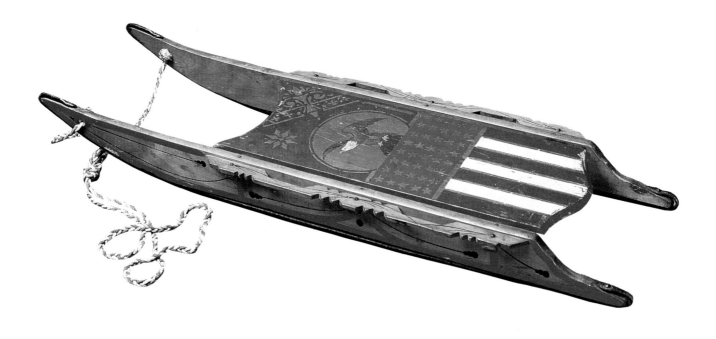

Child's sled, pine with iron runners; New England, 1870–1900. The painted and stenciled decoration includes both the flag and the eagle. The traditional form of the flag has been modified to suit the sled's surface. Folk artists did not hesitate to alter the form of the flag to achieve their purpose, and such alterations were not regarded as improper by their audience.

The flag, of course, was spared, and its stature grew with the tradition that even those who opposed it could not bring themselves to defile it.

For Americans, the flag became, like the eagle and Uncle Sam, grist for the creative folk art mill. Weathervanes were shaped in its form; other vane figures, such as Columbia or the goddess of Liberty, clasp it in their hands. The 1893 catalog published by J. W. Fiske of New York City illustrated a flag-bearing goddess of Liberty in painted and gilded copper that could be obtained in two sizes: twenty-four or thirty-six inches tall, at a cost of $30 and $45 respectively. A decade earlier, A. B. and W. T. Westervelt, also of New York City, had published a catalog that offered the goddess in similar sizes as well as in a large, forty-eight-inch version that could be had for $75.

Westervelt also offered a vane in the form of the flag alone. This was available in sizes ranging from twelve to thirty-six inches in height and cost $12, $18, or $30. Flag vanes were either unpopular or very fragile, for they are extremely rare today.

And, of course, the flag was an important element of many whirligigs. Aptly termed wind toys, these were made to be set up where the wind could turn their paddlelike arms. Spinning in the sun atop a shed or fence post, whirligigs offered many American children their first glimpse of the national colors. Artistic license might alter the traditional form of Old Glory, as in the example shown here in which a bugler salutes a stylized flag that has a single star set within a field of stripes.

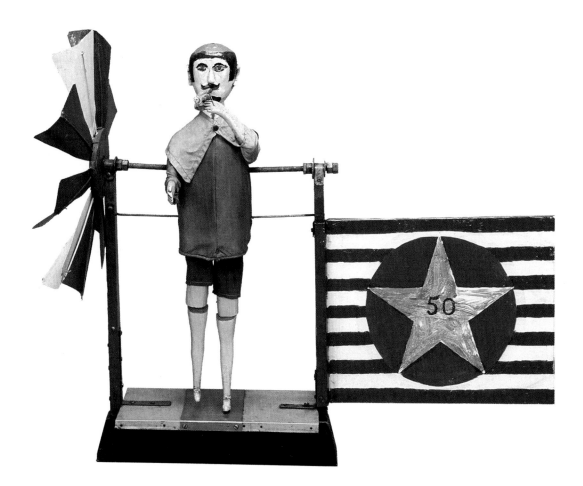

Smaller whirligigs such as the popular sailor and soldier forms with their revolving arms would often bear a flag in each hand. These might be carved from wood or made from tin or stiff paper joined to a wooden staff.

For the particularly patriotic, the flag might become an architectural element. Probably the best known of such examples is the famous flag gate owned by the Museum of American Folk Art. Made in Jefferson County, New York, about the time of the 1876 centennial, this remarkable piece has vertical slats cut in a rippling manner to convey the impression of a banner blowing in the wind.

It is known that doors and even fireboards—solid pieces of wood placed before a fireplace opening during summer months to prevent the entry of leaves, dust, and lost birds—were painted to resemble the national colors. However, such exuberance was no doubt limited by concern that no disrespect be shown the flag.

For the sake of art or expediency, these folk art renditions of the banner are often inexact in detail, particularly as the inclusion of more states increased the number of stars in the field. But this made little difference, for the evocative power remained.

The flag was displayed on every public occasion, particularly on those associated with the great struggle for freedom from British rule. Thus, an article in the *Hempstead Inquirer* of July 8, 1835, began with the statement:

"The fifty-ninth anniversary of our national independence was

Whirligig in the form of a bugler, wood, iron, tin, and painted cloth; New York, ca. 1950. The bugler is a common patriotic motif symbolizing the awakening of the nation at signs of danger. The use of red, white, and blue on the propeller blades extends the concept of the flag into a new dimension.

The Circus Arrives in Town, oil on canvas; by Janis Price, Ohio, 1986. The contemporary folk artist has captured the excitement caused by the arrival of a traveling circus in a small town. The abundance of flags in the scene reflects the fact that the circus was offered as patriotic entertainment; indeed, for many Americans during the 19th and early 20th centuries, attending the circus was a patriotic gesture.

ABOVE: Tavern sign, painted pine; from Centreville, Pennsylvania, ca. 1865. Until well into the 19th century, hotels and taverns announced their presence with large, brightly decorated signs. As in this case, many displayed the national colors or some other indication of the proprietor's patriotism. This piece was signed by its maker, a certain Richardson. Unfortunately, nothing more is known of him. OPPOSITE TOP: Barn door archway decoration, pine with traces of white paint; Connecticut, 1880–1915. This architectural fragment once crowned the doorway to a rural barn. An important part of the American flag, the star was eagerly adopted by folk artists as a decorative motif. OPPOSITE BOTTOM: Washboard, cast iron; Midwest, 1880–1910. This star-decorated washboard was undoubtedly durable, but its weight must have proven too much for most women, and the type is extremely rare today.

celebrated in this village in a manner and with a spirit becoming the occasion. At sunrise our national banner was unfurled to the breeze and a salute of twenty-four guns was fired."

Other gatherings and festivities provided opportunities to display the flag. Traveling circuses could always be counted on to include the national banner not only in its customary form but also as carved and painted decoration for the side panels of circus wagons, on carousel horses, and on the various ancillary structures, such as sideshow buildings. Most examples of such folk carving and painting are now gone, making the pieces that remain particularly valuable fragments of something once common.

The flag sometimes appears in unexpected places. Common stoneware storage crocks were sometimes embellished with one or more flags, sometimes accompanied by piles of cannonballs or an eagle; this custom was particularly common about the time of the 1876 centennial. The example shown here is probably a bit earlier, as the addition of the word *Union* raises the possibility that it was made at the time of or soon after the Civil War, when "Union" was a rallying cry for the Northern forces. The decoration is in blue, as is almost always the case since the mineral that produced the color, cobalt, was one of the two coloring agents that could stand the high temperatures at which stoneware was fired (the other mineral, manganese, produced an unappealing dark brown).

Patriotism was one of the first lessons of the young, and children's

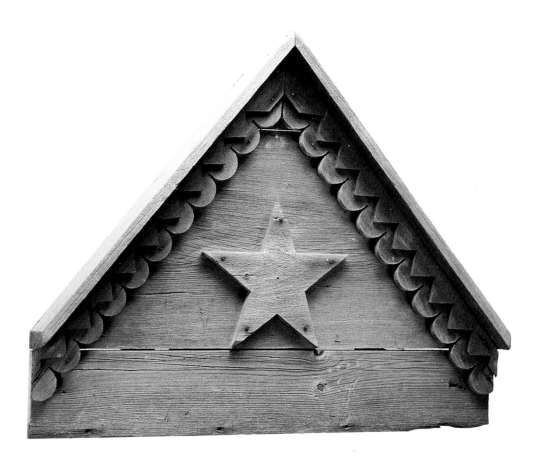

toys often incorporated the flag as a decorative element. In the sled illustrated here, the stars and bars (along with the eagle) form the body decoration. Apparently, it was not regarded as improper to sit on the flag! The flag's colors were also incorporated in puzzles, building blocks, numerous books, and games, so that by the time a child reached maturity, he or she had become thoroughly familiar with them.

Later on, as an adult, one might purchase a wide variety of foodstuffs and useful objects packed in or, should we say, "wrapped" in the flag. There was a not-so-subtle message to such advertising. After all, because Americans loved and respected the national colors, a canister of tea, a tin box of cookies, or even a pint of whiskey that was decorated with Old Glory would for many Americans somehow seem to be of superior quality.

The elements of the sovereign banner were also utilized in decoration. Most often seen was the national shield, which might include both stars and stripes or only the latter. Such unlikely items as cast-iron stove plates, fraternal symbols, and the top hats worn by those taking part in political parades could be given this particular flourish.

The stars and stripes of the flag were frequently used independently. Stars appeared as decorative motifs on such homespun objects as cast-iron warming plates for coal stoves, washboards, game boards, and architectural elements.

The flag's stripes often supplemented those of the barber pole,

TOP: Utility box, painted pine with incised six-pointed stars; Pennsylvania, 1850–1900. With its unusual cutout handle and interesting compartmentation, this piece was probably a labor of love, made as a gift to a family member who would appreciate not only the thought but the patriotic motifs used in the design. ABOVE: Storage box, walnut or hickory with notch-carved decoration and inlay including a five-pointed star; Maine, 1850–80. This piece shows careful construction, particularly the relief-carved trailing vine that encircles the exterior sides. Identifying the makers of such pieces is seldom possible, as few are signed.

the traditional colors of which—alternating red and white—reflect the fact that in years past the barber was also a "leech," or bleeder, rendering rudimentary medical treatment: barbers hung their bloody red bandages on poles outside their places of business. The American barber, today as in the past, often sports a pole that is red, white, and blue, colors not seen displayed on the poles in front of European tonsorial establishments.

As the fledgling nation spread its wings, it carried the colors abroad. Figureheads, sternboards, and other carved and decorated portions of warships and merchantmen bore the red, white, and blue. Sailors in foreign ports hired native craftsmen to create large needlework pictures incorporating the flag, the eagle, a watercolor of their ship, and, of course, a personal portrait—all to be brought home in triumph years later and displayed upon the parlor wall. Likewise of non-American origin, but folk art nonetheless, were the boxed shellwork pictures and sailor's valentines, some of which linked the flag with names of loved ones and ports of call.

Paintings of the flag and paintings in which the flag appears are legion. At one time, many signs that hung over taverns or stores or marked the entrance to rural communities proudly displayed the colors, reflecting the unquestioned patriotic enthusiasm of the owners, proprietors, or residents.

Folk artists were equally devoted. Since flags were once a com-

Game board, painted pine; New York, 1900–20. This game board was designed for the popular game of Chinese checkers, which is played with marbles on a playing surface in the shape of a six-pointed star. This interesting piece has the visual appeal so dear to collectors of American folk art.

mon sight on battlefields, few 19th-century American military paintings fail to contain one or more representations of the Republic's banner. Even today, contemporary folk artists may fill a canvas with a dozen or more flags; a good example is Milton Bond's *Allied Victory Parade, 1918*.

This enthusiasm for the flag has been shared by collectors of American folk art and has also, unfortunately, given rise to a form of fakery that involves "touching up" a perfectly fine painting with one or more flags in an effort to increase its value. Thus, a 19th-century painting of an unidentified sailing ship or a ship bearing an English or French flag becomes much more salable through the addition of Old Glory. The same may be true of a simple landscape with a few houses. Thousands of such works were made during the 1800s, but very few show buildings with flags. If one or two flags are added, the price will often increase a dozenfold.

Collectors are becoming aware of such shenanigans, and most sophisticated enthusiasts now include a black light among their equipment when going to view paintings. Under this ultraviolet light, the newly added paint will appear different from the original, revealing the added work.

Much "flag" art was created by men, but women never lagged behind in patriotic fervor. Since the early 19th century, the flag has served as central motif for lavish quilt constructions, and hooked rugs may also feature Old Glory. The charming rug shown here features a scene at the village train station, for years the focal point of communities fortunate enough to claim one. Dominating the composition is a large building (probably the engine house) from which flies a freely adapted version of the Stars and Stripes.

Equally appealing is the flag quilt, entitled "Stars and Stripes Forever," illustrated on the dust jacket of this book. Created for the Great American Quilt Festival of 1986 by Jane F. Cahan of Clayton, Missouri, this remarkable textile *tour de force* indicates the patriotism of its designer and also dramatically illustrates that quilt-making skills are alive and well in present-day U.S.A.

Both quilts and hooked rugs were made in abundance for the celebrations of the 1876 centennial and the 1976 bicentennial. It is inspiring to see that many of the patriotic motifs popular in 1876 were repeated in work done a century later.

An unusual and not often seen use of the flag was in patriotic costumes made to be worn by those taking part in parades and pageants associated with holidays like the Fourth of July and Washington's birthday. It was not regarded as disrespectful to adapt the flag's stars, stripes, and colors to articles of clothing. Thus, men frequently appeared at such festivities clad in pants striped red and white or red,

OPPOSITE: Barber pole, painted pine; Northeast, 1875–1900. The traditional red and white stripes reflect the barber's former role of "leech," a surgeon who drew blood to "cure" sundry ailments. Out of patriotic enthusiasm, American barbers sometimes add blue stripes or even stars to their poles. ABOVE: *Allied Victory Parade, 1918*, reverse-glass painting; by Milton Bond, Connecticut, 1984. Bond, a contemporary folk painter working in an unusual medium, captures the enthusiasm of the victorious nation, particularly evident in the great number of flags that flew from buildings along the parade route.

Quilt, cotton with appliqué design; probably from Pennsylvania, 1888. This unusual quilt features a complete train, railway line, and station as well as a horse and buggy, house, and penned cow. The station house is crowned with a flag, a common scene in the 19th century, when nearly all public and many private buildings flew the colors. The flag here has been modified by the artist.

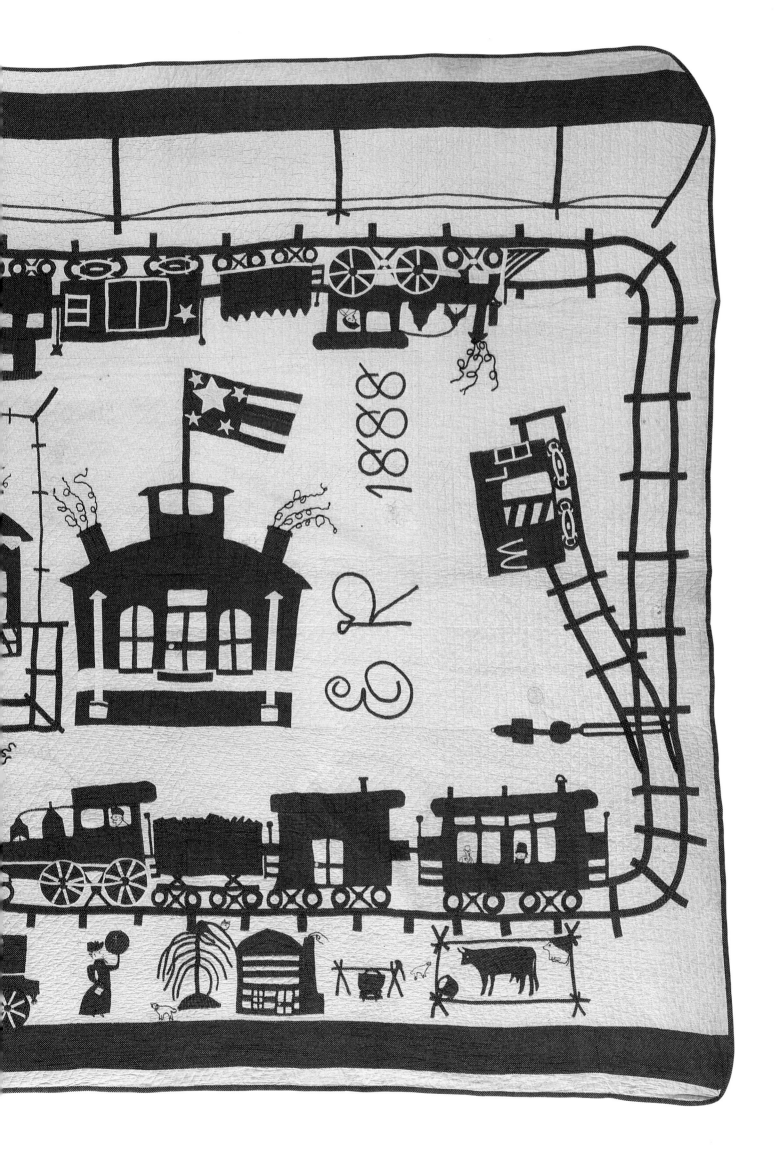

Storage jar, salt-glazed stoneware with cobalt-blue decoration of American flags and stacked cannonballs; New York or Pennsylvania, 1860–70. The word *Union* on this piece suggests that it dates to the Civil War period. Such pottery was usually made to fill a special order or as a gift rather than for general sale.

white, and blue to accompany star-speckled vests and flag-decked top hats. Women would create whole gowns in the form of the national colors, in effect mimicking Liberty, who was often depicted draped in the flag.

Other patriotic textiles that display the flag include handkerchiefs and scarves. Some of these were made at home by clever seamstresses; others were produced in factories. An example of the latter is the large political banner promoting the unsuccessful 1884 presidential candidacy of James G. Blaine. On a somewhat smaller scale are the silken squares that were given away as premiums in tobacco packages. Many of these bore renditions of the American flag, and these were sometimes incorporated by quilt makers in the crazy quilts—quilts made of scraps of silk, satin, and velvet seamed together and bound over with elaborate embroidery stitches—so popular in the late 19th century.

The importance of the flag as a symbol of national unity cannot be underestimated in a country so large and culturally diversified as ours, and it seems likely that folk artists will continue to utilize this motif.

Detail of quilt (page 8) made of printed centennial commemorative kerchiefs; United States, ca. 1876. This detail is of the American flag and the flags of other nations participating in the celebration; other kerchiefs used in the quilt illustrate George Washington, the Declaration of Independence, and the Memorial Hall Art Gallery at the centennial grounds.

Surrender at Nashville, oil on Masonite; by Albert Webster Davies, New Hampshire, ca. 1960. The Civil War has inspired many generations of American folk artists. As in most works related to war, the national standard appears in a prominent position. Davies is better known for romantic landscapes than for paintings of violence like this.

THE ORIGINAL AMERICANS

Given the long, ambiguous, and very often hostile relationship between whites and native Americans, it is not surprising that native Americans should figure prominently in American folk art. Initially, the original inhabitants of America—already called Indians, a result of Columbus's conviction that he had arrived in the Indies—appeared as illustrations in the journals and on the maps made by early explorers. These works, usually watercolors, are extremely rare today and are generally found only in museum collections.

Despite their relatively primitive level of culture, the members of the various tribes were almost always portrayed in such a way as to suggest their unique characteristics—and their nobility. They stood straight and tall, were almost regally dressed, and while they showed certain European characteristics in both clothing and accoutrements, they were clearly exotic.

The curiosity and even compassion evidenced in such 16th- and 17th-century works vanished as conflicts grew between the races, and it was not until the mid 19th century—by which time the Indian had been driven far enough west that he had become for most Americans a distant symbol rather than a source of terror—that the Indian again emerged as a sympathetic figure. His role at this point was commercial: the promotion of products, primarily tobacco and proprietary medicines, made and sold by whites.

Tobacco is native to the New World, and the native Americans were the first to cultivate and use it. Once Europeans began to smoke,

Advertising poster, lithographed paper; made for Dr. Morse's Indian Root Pills, 1890–1900. Honored as natural healers whose secret herbal medicines exceeded the curative powers of white medicine, Indians were often used in advertising patent medicines.

they began to cast about for ways to advertise both the leaf and the tobacco shops through which it was sold. The figure of a black was first used, reflecting the role slaves played in the cultivation of the crop, but by the mid 19th century, the Indian had emerged as the traditional tobacconist's symbol.

From about 1840 until the early 1900s, carvers such as the well-known New York craftsmen Samuel Robb and Charles J. Dodge turned out a variety of finely crafted life-size figures. These were usually mounted on wheels so that they could be rolled into place outside the shop in the morning and then retired again in the evening.

The traditional form is that of an Indian chief clasping a bundle of tobacco leaves in one hand, but many variations exist. For example, the brave may grasp a knife, rifle, spear, pipe, hatchet, or bow and arrows in the other hand.

Squaws also appear, usually offering a handful of cigars, tobacco leaves, or a cigar box. Matched couples are rare; also uncommon are counter-sized examples only two or three feet tall.

The quality of the carving varies greatly. A comparison of the two examples shown here reveals that one—the squaw—is extremely well carved, with outstanding detail and such interesting touches as the use of tobacco leaves to form her headdress, while the other is quite crude.

By the turn of the century, manufacturers such as Demuth of New York were casting these figures in zinc. There were good reasons for this change in materials. Old carving traditions were dying out, and it was becoming harder and harder to find craftsmen capable of producing sophisticated and appealing figures. Moreover, industrial pollution and hard usage in larger communities made short work of painted wood.

A cast-metal figure was more durable, could be repainted countless times, and was much less expensive to manufacture, since any number of duplicates could be cast from a single mold. Of course, such repetition soon loses any artistic pretensions, and the zinc tobacconist's figures were probably no more appealing to those who saw them daily on the streets than they are to most contemporary collectors. In any case, they were the last of the breed.

By 1930, the traditional cigar-store Indian had largely vanished from American streets. Several factors led to the disappearance of the cigar-store Indian. Increasing literacy made all shop figures less essential than they had been. Also, the widening of streets, particularly in larger communities, and the increased vehicular traffic (especially when the automobile made its appearance), made trade signs something of a nuisance. Finally, at least in the West, lingering hostility toward the Indian played a part. In one Wyoming cow town, it became necessary to remove cigar-store Indians from the street because cowboys, in town for a Saturday night "toot," had a habit of shooting at them, endangering both the property and the lives of the townsfolk.

The figures of native Americans also frequently appeared on bottles of patent, or proprietary, medicines because of the belief that, as expounded in the *Kickapoo Almanac* of 1896:

"The Noble Savage was . . . a better curative agent than the youth, who after a dozen medical lectures or so . . . is given authority as an M.D. to try his hand on anybody who comes along."

The patent medicine poster illustrated here is a particularly good example of the genre. The Indian, strong and healthy, mounted on horseback and armed with his primitive but effective weapons, is seen in combat with the great grizzly bear, symbol of the raw, untamed wilderness. The Indian's imminent triumph will, without doubt, be due to his "good medicine."

The notion that Indians knew how to employ natural herbs and techniques to cure illnesses beyond the care of what passed in the 19th century for scientific medicine persisted in the concept of faith healing and botanical medicine. It also led to the manufacture of numerous pseudomedicines, such as Indian Compound of Honey Boneset, Mountain Herb Pills, Indian Salve, Dr. Morse's Indian Root Pills, and Dr. Kilmer's Indian Cough Cure. While the embossed bottles are often quite lovely, the medicine was usually about 70 percent alcohol, sometimes with a dash of opium thrown in!

Native Americans also appeared on weathervanes and whirligigs. Fraternal organizations, such as the I.O.O.F. and the Improved Order of Red Men, commissioned giant, six to eight foot tall figures to place atop their lodge halls. Smaller, copper, iron, or tin vanes were used on private homes.

The sheet-iron weathervane illustrated here is a particularly dramatic example. Found in New England and dating from the 19th century, it shows the "red man" in his most fearsome image, with tomahawk held high and bow at hand. Of course, by the time this piece was made, the few Indians left in the area had long ceased to be a threat. It is unlikely that such a vane would have graced a Massachusetts or Vermont rooftop during the 17th or 18th centuries!

The whirligig form most often seen is that of an Indian rowing a canoe; the paddle arms turn in the wind. Less common is the brave who clasps a tomahawk in each hand; the broad surfaces of the tomahawks' blades are exposed to the vagrant breezes. Both types were made during the 19th century, but most examples are of more recent vintage. In fact, directions for making the canoe-type whirligig appeared in issues of *Popular Mechanics* magazine during the 1930s and 1940s.

The Indian also often graced trade signs, particularly those adver-

OPPOSITE: Tobacconist's figure, carved and painted wood; by Samuel Robb, New York City, 1875–1900. Robb was one of the most important carvers of trade figures. This example is known as "Rose Squaw" because she holds a rose in her hand, supposedly a symbol for Robb's deceased wife. ABOVE: Tobacconist's figure, carved and painted wood with brass details; Massachusetts, 1900–20. When this relatively crude piece was made, the cigar-store Indian was vanishing from America's streets. Even so, it conforms in general to examples made fifty years earlier.

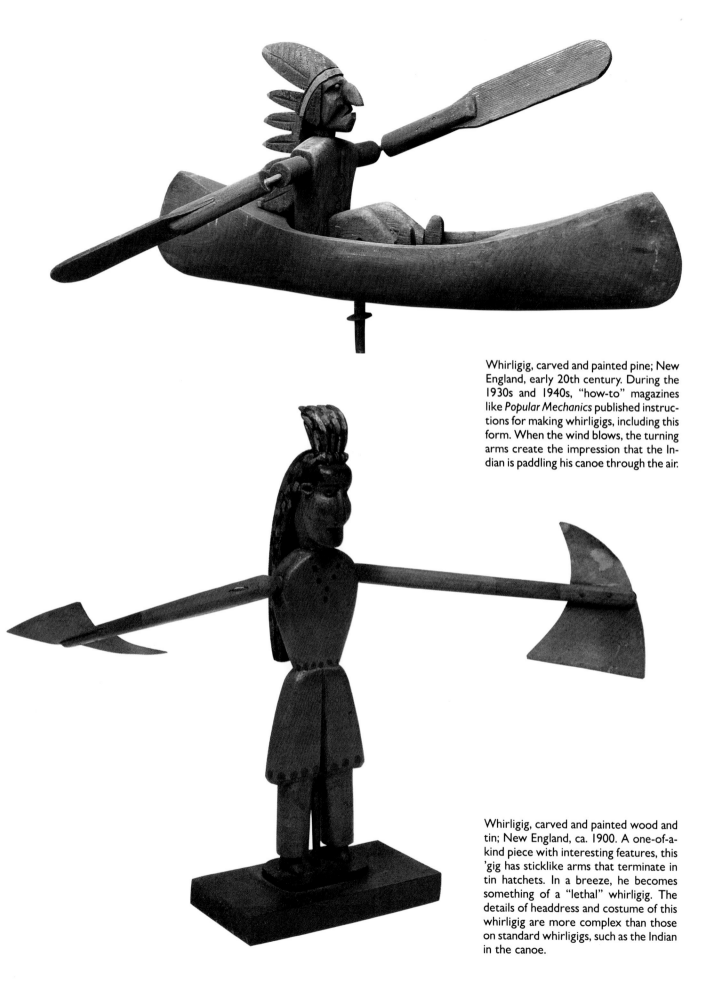

Whirligig, carved and painted pine; New England, early 20th century. During the 1930s and 1940s, "how-to" magazines like *Popular Mechanics* published instructions for making whirligigs, including this form. When the wind blows, the turning arms create the impression that the Indian is paddling his canoe through the air.

Whirligig, carved and painted wood and tin; New England, ca. 1900. A one-of-a-kind piece with interesting features, this 'gig has sticklike arms that terminate in tin hatchets. In a breeze, he becomes something of a "lethal" whirligig. The details of headdress and costume of this whirligig are more complex than those on standard whirligigs, such as the Indian in the canoe.

Tobacconist's figure, carved and painted oak with clay pipe; England or the United States, 1790–1820. Trade figures were common in stores and on streets during most of the 19th century. This figure probably represents a West Indian. Only three feet tall, it was made to stand on a counter.

Sitting Bull, oil on canvas; by Larry Zingale, New York, 1982. Zingale is fascinated by the nation's first inhabitants. Here he captures the power and character of one of the great Indian leaders.

Indian Woman, oil on canvas; by Larry Zingale, New York, 1976. A major contemporary folk artist, Zingale was originally a landscape painter, but in the past decade he has turned to portraits, including those of native Americans.

ABOVE: Kachina, carved and painted cottonwood; Hopi, 1890–1900. This figure represents the deity Lakone Mana, one of over one thousand such deities inhabiting the Hopi pantheon. Kachina figures served to educate Indian children in tribal beliefs. ABOVE RIGHT: Doll, buckskin with beadwork moccasins, belt, and cape; plains Indians, 1900–10. Few Indian playthings from this period can be found, making this doll a rare survivor. A particular authenticity is added to this piece by the fact that it is equipped with a human-hair wig. BELOW RIGHT: Examples of plains Indians beadwork; gauntlets or wristlets, gloves, and cuffs. Thousands of tiny glass "seed beads" may be used in a single piece of native American beadwork. Before these beads were available in trade from whites, similar work was done with porcupine quills.

tising country resorts and mountain hideaways—the Indian's celebrated knowledge of the forest was thus used to guarantee the authenticity of the sylvan location. In the example illustrated here, a caricature of a brave climbs a pine tree and peers out over the thick forest that, no doubt, surrounds Woodtop Resort. This painted-sheet-iron sign was probably made in the early 1900s and was used to mark the entrance to an eastern or upper midwestern summer camp.

Less often encountered are pieces of 19th-century redware and stoneware bearing Indian heads or complete Indian figures. In most cases, these date to before 1850 and were usually decorated by incising the form into the soft clay prior to firing. Sometimes, the figure is also outlined in color. At a much later period—from about 1906 to 1937—the Western Stoneware Company of Monmouth, Illinois, produced the famous "Old Sleepy Eye" line of molded pottery, featuring pitchers, mugs, bowls, and crocks bearing an embossed image said to be that of Chief Sleepy Eyes (Ish-tak-ha-ba) of the Sisseton Sioux, whose tribe once occupied the land around Sleepy Eye, Minnesota.

Other arts paying homage to the native American include that of the toy maker. Nineteenth-century examples include bows and arrows, painted shields, and miniature feather headdresses. During the 1930s, the Grey Iron Casting Company of Mount Joy, Pennsylvania, turned out a variety of Indian figures, both standing and mounted. The cast-iron specimens illustrated here include a scout and two chiefs wearing feathered headdresses.

Although native Americans were and are expert weavers, they seldom appear on textiles made by whites. Indians do appear on a few pieces of white tatting work and on some hooked rugs, but the image of an Indian is only rarely found on quilts and samplers.

The folk crafts of the American Indian are, of course, legion—the Indians made by hand everything they needed. The western plains tribes, such as the Sioux, produced magnificent beadwork-decorated hide blankets, gloves, skirts, shirts, and moccasins, with flowers, geometric patterns, and human figures all formed from tiny glass trade beads obtained in barter with the whites. The examples shown here are typical of the high quality achieved by these artisans.

Beadwork was also used to decorate the deerskin dolls that Indian parents made for their children. Though most such pieces seen today were made within the past several decades for sale to tourists, late-19th- and early 20th-century dolls in museum collections include examples from such widely disparate sources as the Cheyenne, Seminole, Navajo, and Seneca. The doll illustrated here was produced by one of the plains Indian tribes during the period 1900 to 1910. Its buckskin body is heavily decorated with beadwork and human hair.

Many native Americans created basketry, and basket making was

ABOVE: Basket or olla, woven grass; Southwest, 1900–20. Native Americans are regarded as among the world's finest basket makers. Geometric designs and abstract representations of humans and animals mark the best examples of their craft. FOLLOWING PAGES: *Indian Camp*, acrylic on canvas; by Kathy Jakobsen, New York City, 1983. Many contemporary folk painters are drawn to the subject of native Americans. This view of an Indian village captures the sense of tranquility that must have often pervaded such settlements.

ABOVE: Trade sign, painted sheet steel; New England or Midwest, 1900–30. Woodtop was probably a private camp located in a mountain area, and the Indian peering from the treetop lookout was intended as a humorous comment on life in the woods. Native Americans seldom find such depictions amusing. OPPOSITE TOP: Toy Indians, painted cast iron; Grey Iron Casting Company, Mount Joy, Pennsylvania, 1930–40. The wood and papier-mâché campfire with brass kettle and chain is from the same period. Though never as popular as military figures, cowboys and Indians have been made as playthings since the early 1900s. Most are of lead or pot metal, though examples in wood, cardboard, and papier-mâché can also be found. OPPOSITE BOTTOM: Weathervane, sheet iron; New England, late 19th century. This powerful and stylish figure depicts the "red man" as many New Englanders once saw him—as a strong and fearsome adversary, very different from the almost cartoonlike character he came to be in some 20th-century depictions.

brought to an especially high level by such southwestern tribes as the Navajo, Apache, and Pima and by the Pit River, Klamath, Makah, and Modoc tribes of the northwestern coastal region.

These containers were remarkable not only for their strength and durability—some were waterproof, and others could be used to heat food over a fire—but also for their artistry. Their geometric designs, usually in black on a lighter ground, incorporated abstract human and animal figures as well as symbols relating to complex religious beliefs.

Though sometimes mistakenly identified as dolls or toys, the famous kachina figures made by the Hopi of the Southwest were actually representations of religious deities used in instructing children in tribal myths. These remarkable carved and painted forms come in a wide variety. The Lakone Mana kachina illustrated here dates to the turn of the century. Collector interest in such works has reached the point where examples made by contemporary carvers may cost over a thousand dollars, and roadside stands throughout the western states are often filled with plastic replicas made in Taiwan.

Over the past few years, contemporary white folk artists have been turning more and more to the production of images of native Americans, reflecting in their work the new respect shown for the first Americans. Such well-known painters as Kathy Jakobsen are exploring the lives and stories of the various Indian tribes and setting down their histories on canvas.

My Desert, carved and painted wood; by John Cisney, Minnesota, 1986. Cisney sees the native American in terms of his environment, surrounded by cacti, animals, and the symbols of his faith.

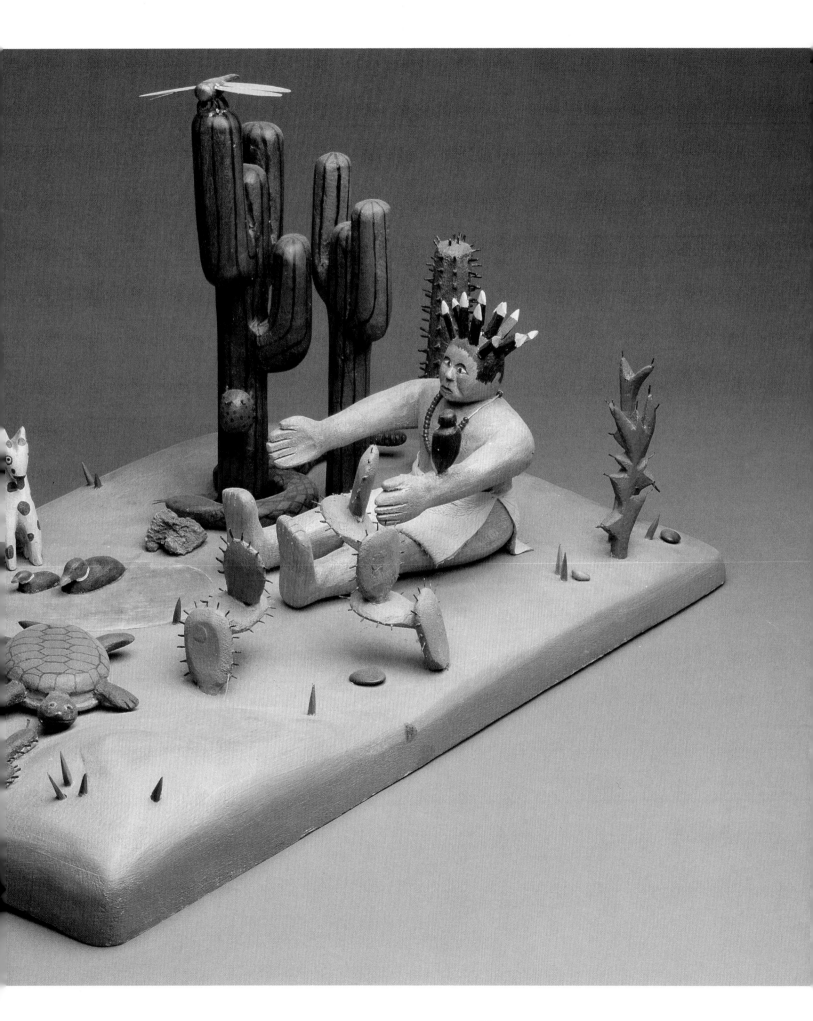

Portrait of an Indian, watercolor on paper; by Daniel H. Reese, made for a lodge of the Improved Order of Red Men at Nanticoke, Pennsylvania, early 20th century. Native Americans appear frequently in American folk painting, but they are especially popular in connection with various secret societies that adopted the Indian as symbol.

On Lookout Mountain, oil on canvas; by Sylvia Alberts, New York City and Maine, 1974. A Manhattan resident fascinated by ethnic types, Alberts here poses a family on a precarious rock perch at Lookout Mountain, Georgia.

S. ALBERTS

FATHERS OF THE NATION

Just as America's folk artists have turned for inspiration to the symbols of their new nation, so have they extolled the men and women through whose sacrifice and efforts freedom was achieved. First and foremost of these was George Washington, whose life gave rise both to popular myths—such as the Potomac River coin toss and the youthful chopping down of a cherry tree—and to myriad folk portraits. Not until the period of John F. Kennedy was there again such a demand for presidential likenesses, and in some homes these very nearly assumed the role of religious icons.

Washington, known as the Father of His Country even during his own lifetime, tried hard to resist the attempts to venerate both his person and the office of president. He rebuffed John Adams's wish to attach to the president such European and undemocratic titles as "His Highness" and refused to allow his likeness to appear on the first U.S. coins. Even so, Washington spent much of the later years of his life posing for artists. That he was not always delighted with this occupation is evident from the following comments he made in a 1785 letter:

"I am so hackneyed to the touches of the painter's pencil that I am now altogether at their beck, and sit like 'Patience on a monument' while they are delineating the lines of my face. It is proof, among many others, of what habit and custom may accomplish; at first I was impatient at the request, and as restive under the operation as a colt is under the saddle; the next time I submitted very reluctantly, but with less flouncing; now no dray-horse moves more readily to his thrill than I to

Portrait of Abraham Lincoln, painted relief-carved wood with a background of red, white, and blue stripes; by Elijah Pierce, Columbus, Ohio, ca. 1975. Pierce specializes in religious subjects, but like many black artists, he has a particular fondness for Lincoln, whom he portrays in a strongly sympathetic manner.

Toy train passenger coach, the "President," cast iron; Ives, Blakeslee & Williams, Bridgeport, Connecticut, ca. 1895. Railway cars, both full-size and toy, were frequently named for presidents and other important political and military figures.

the painter's chair." (Rufus Wilmot Griswold, *The Republican Court, or American Society in the Days of Washington*, 1855)

New England folk portraits of the first president were usually straightforward likenesses based generally on similar academic work. Sometimes, as in the reverse-glass paintings of the Prior-Hamblen school (an example of which is shown on page 65), Martha would join George in a dual portrait; sometimes she appeared alone in a matching portrait.

Pennsylvania fraktur painters delighted in more robust depictions of Washington. The general can be seen upon his horse, sword in hand, pointing toward enemy lines. These watercolors derived from similar Germanic examples (many include a text lettered by hand in a style similar to the 16th-century typeface called Fraktur; hence the name).

Washington's death, in 1799, had a profound effect on the American people. The man who in life had labored so hard to avoid being treated as royalty was very nearly sanctified in death. Portraits of Washington, already in demand, increased in popularity. The national veneration of the great leader was noted by foreign visitors. Following a visit to this country in 1811, the Russian diplomat Paul Svinin wrote, "It is noteworthy that every American considers it his sacred duty to have a likeness of Washington in his home, just as we have images of God's saints."

Women created painted or needleworked mourning pictures, or memorials, that featured a tomb inscribed with the deceased presi-

dent's name and perhaps a line or two extolling his virtues, several mourners, usually including one or more Revolutionary War soldiers, and a figure of Columbia or Liberty. The inscription on one such picture reads:

"Sacred to the Memory of the truly Illustrious George Washington, Renowned in War, Great in the Senate, and possessed of every Qualification to render him worthy [of] the Title of a Great and Good man."

In fact, following Washington's death, mourning became patriotic—and fashionable. In addition to portraits or mourning pictures of Washington, few American homes were without mourning pictures celebrating occasions of more personal tragedy—the death of a loved one or even the demise of a pet or the termination of a romantic involvement. The effect such highly sentimental works might have on an impressionable youth is recorded in Mark Twain's *The Adventures of Huckleberry Finn* (1884), in which young Huck finds himself in a typical American home:

"They had pictures hung on the walls—mainly Washingtons and Lafayettes, and battles . . . and one called 'Signing the Declaration.' There was some that they called crayons, which one of the daughters which was dead made her own self when she was only fifteen years old. They was different from any pictures I ever see before; blacker, mostly, than is common. One was a woman in a slim black dress, belted small under the arm-pits, with bulges like a cabbage in the middle of the

Pull toy locomotive, the "U.S. Grant," turned and painted wood with lithographed paper decoration; New York or New England, 1890–1910. Not only is this toy named after the illustrious leader, but visible through the window is the great Grant himself, serving as engineer.

ABOVE: Portrait of George Washington in pencil, ink, and crayon on paper; United States, 1932. Created by an unknown folk artist on the occasion of the two-hundredth anniversary of Washington's birth, this portrait is probably taken from a print. OPPOSITE: *General George Washington*, pencil, pen, and watercolor; probably from Pennsylvania, 1830–50. In the tradition of Pennsylvania fraktur paintings, this piece shows great detail and a fine sense of color. It is a masterful example of the folk art genre.

General George Washington.

Uncle Sam, carved and painted wood; by Bryan McNutt, Collegville, Texas, 1986. McNutt is well known for his "life-size" versions of Uncle Sam. Created in honor of the centennial of the Statue of Liberty, this figure bears an eagle on its right arm, and *Liberty* is painted on the base.

sleeves, and a large black scoop-shovel bonnet with a black veil, and white slim ankles crossed about with black tape, and very wee black slippers, like a chisel, and she was leaning pensive on a tombstone on her right elbow, under a weeping willow, and her other hand hanging down her side holding a white handkerchief and a reticule, and underneath the picture it said 'Shall I Never See Thee More Alas.' Another one was a young lady with her hair all combed up straight to the top of her head, and knotted there in front of a comb like a chair-back, and she was crying into a handkerchief and had a dead bird laying on its back in her other hand with its heels up, and underneath the picture it said 'I Shall Never Hear Thy Sweet Chirrup More Alas.' There was one where a young lady was at a window looking up at the moon, and tears running down her cheeks; and she had an open letter in one hand with black sealing-wax showing on one edge of it, and she was mashing a locket with a chain to it against her mouth, and underneath the picture it said 'And Art Thou Gone Yes Thou Art Gone Alas.' These was all nice pictures, I reckon, but I didn't somehow seem to take to them, because if ever I was down a little, they always give me the fantods."

While possibly based on somewhat earlier English prints, these memorials were a unique American contribution to the world of folk art, Huck's fantods notwithstanding.

The makers of Berlin work patterns also profited from the national craving for images of the great leader. Not all of these representations were well received. In *Life on the Mississippi* (1883), Mark Twain, evidently something of a needlework critic, described a Berlin work piece entitled "Washington Crossing the Delaware" as "done in thunder-and-lightning crewels by one of the young ladies—work of art which would have made Washington hesitate about crossing, if he could have foreseen what advantage was going to be taken of it."

The first president was a popular subject matter for other textile forms, including quilts, hooked rugs, woven coverlets, and small pieces used to decorate tabletops and other furnishings. In most instances, particularly in the case of coverlets, only a bust of the general would appear. Some makers, however, such as the New York State coverlet weaver James Cunningham, embellished their pieces with equestrian figures of Washington. Lest there be any doubt as to the identity of the horseman riding across his coverlets, Cunningham wove the name "Washington" and the motto "United We Stand, Divided We Fall" beneath the figure.

The tomb of the fallen commander took on its own significance, appearing in 19th-century watercolors and sandpaper paintings at the very time it was falling into disrepair. In his *Voyage to America*, Thomas Cather painted a rather gloomy picture of his visit to Washington's tomb:

Candy container in the form of Uncle Sam, cardboard with applied lithographed paper decoration; made for the Fanny Farmer candy company, 1930–50. Given as party favors, such containers came in many different forms and were usually filled with sugar candies or jelly beans. This container's movable arms suggest that it could also be used as a toy.

RIGHT: Cream pitcher, white earthenware decorated with transfer printed representations of Admiral Dewey and his flagship, the *Olympia*; Cook Pottery Company, Trenton, New Jersey, ca. 1898. Following his victory over the Spanish fleet at Manila Bay, Dewey was embraced by the American populace with almost hysterical enthusiasm, and his image appeared everywhere, from numerous folk paintings to the sides of cream pitchers. Note that the spout is in the form of an eagle. BELOW RIGHT: Figural pitcher in the shape of President Herbert Hoover, yellowware; Syracuse China Company, Syracuse, New York, 1929–33. A facsimile of the president's signature appears on the base. Probably made in limited numbers during the term of an increasingly unpopular chief executive, these pitchers are now rare.

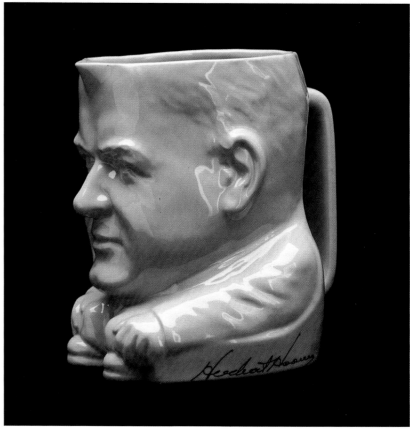

"April 11th, 1836. Drove to Mount Vernon, a lovely spot, but sadly neglected. . . .The place appears to have been allowed to go wild, untouched by the hand of a man since the death of its illustrious proprietor. . . . There was an air of extreme melancholy and loneliness in the deserted appearance of the garden. The gate, old and rickety, was creaking in every blast. . . . In a little dell near the house, in the shade of some cedar trees, is the grave of Washington. It is a simple vault surrounded by a brick wall. Over the gate is the inscription, 'Within this enclosure rest the remains of General George Washington.' As I stood there I felt it is one of the holiest spots on earth, which contains the bones of him who had conferred such benefits on mankind. Freedom's own blessed and glorious champion, the Father of his country, the incorruptible Patriot, the pure statesman, the Good man."

Despite the neglect of his tomb, Washington's countrymen did not forget him, and he appeared throughout the 19th century in a variety of folk guises: on whiskey bottles, his visage often combined with that of a lesser politician seeking public office; on andirons, such as the pair illustrated here; as a whirligig or weathervane; and, of course, on inn signs, on which he kept company with various other illustrious patriots. In her book *A Journey to Ohio in 1810*, Margaret Van Horn Dwight remarked on the proliferation of such heroic advertisements:

"It is quite amusing to see the variety of paintings on the innkeepers' signs. I saw one in N.J. with Thos. Jeff 'n's head and shoulders & his name above it. Today I saw Gen. G Washington, his name underneath [and] Gen. Putnam riding down the steps at Horseneck."

Today, most of the lesser lights of early American history are the subject only of history books, but throughout much of the 19th century, and particularly in New England, the birthdays of such statesmen as Jefferson, Jackson, Hamilton, and the Adamses were noted with local celebrations and the exchange of specially printed post cards. They were also the subjects of portraits, though not as often, of course, as such luminaries as Washington and Lincoln. The watercolor of Andrew Jackson, illustrated here, is a good example. Probably copied from a contemporary print, it portrays the general in old age, but just as feisty as ever.

A highly controversial character, "Old Hickory" was far more popular in his native South than in other areas of the country. His penchant for dueling and his treatment of the Cherokee nation disenchanted many former supporters. Even so, he stood for the common man of the frontier against the entrenched New England aristocracy, a position that foreshadowed the conflict that continues today between the West and the "eastern establishment."

Later figures, such as William Henry Harrison and John Tyler, were immortalized on whiskey bottles or, as in the case of Admiral George

ABOVE: Figurehead likeness of President Ulysses S. Grant, carved and painted pine; Maine, 1865–75. A popular general and controversial president, Grant had many followers. His visage appeared on advertising materials, on toys, and even on painted furniture. This figurehead is graced by especially fine carving. OPPOSITE: Portrait of Andrew Jackson, watercolor, pastels, and pencil on paper; by Ellen T. Harrington, Massachusetts, ca. 1840. Probably adapted from a contemporary print, this folk painting shows great vigor and detail. As is so often the case, little is known of the artist—except that she was only twelve when she created this portrait.

Dewey, hero of Manila Bay, on sugar bowls, creamers, and cups. Even the venerable William Penn lent his reputation for wisdom and prudence—unknowingly, of course—to an insurance company fire mark. This cast-iron marker, issued by the Penn Fire Insurance Company of Pittsburgh around 1845, reflects a common promotional device, the attempt to capitalize on the good reputation of an historical figure in the sale of goods or services.

The nation's children, brought up to recognize and revere the great patriots, were a particularly fertile field for such promotion. Thus, historical figures make frequent appearances in the world of toys. Columbus can be found on a wheel toy cast to resemble the ship from which he alighted to take his first steps on the soil of the New World. President Grant assumes the role of engineer for a wooden locomotive, and thrift was encouraged through the sale of mechanical banks incorporating Washington, Lincoln, or Teddy Roosevelt.

On a more dignified level, folk carvers sculpted busts and full-sized figures of the Founding Fathers that were placed in public buildings and even along streets and highways. Most of these are now gone, but examples of another popular form, the ship figurehead, can still be found. Shown here is a mid-19th-century example bearing the bust of the noble Ulysses S. Grant. Given the undeniable comfort provided the crew, especially of a warship, by the presence on board of such a notable warrior as Grant or Washington, it is not surprising that such figureheads were so popular.

The most important presidential figure following Washington was Abraham Lincoln. Though he was loathed by many of the Americans of his time, his adherents have created a vast body of folk art, including paintings, sculpture, and needlework. Some of the most powerful sculptural forms have come from black artists, who often have portrayed Lincoln as a black or in company with blacks. The painted wooden relief carving shown here was executed by the black artist Elijah Pierce, who was born in Mississippi and lived most of his life in Columbus, Ohio. His works combine strong religious faith with patriotism. His portrait of Lincoln skillfully incorporates elements of the American flag as background.

Twentieth-century folk artists have focused their efforts on the great presidential figures of this century: Franklin D. Roosevelt and John F. Kennedy. Both are the subject of numerous works that with the passage of time will no doubt assume a stature equal to that of earlier art. Other political figures of this era also often appear in caricature, as in the pitcher, illustrated here, depicting President Herbert Hoover as a squat figure compressed into a stylized armchair.

Related to depictions of real-life American heroes are representations of America's legendary characters. One of the best-known of

ANDREW JACKSON.

Pair of George Washington andirons, painted cast iron; New York or New England, 1900–10. These sculptural andirons feature a fine rendition of Washington. Other andirons in the same vein include Hessian soldiers, Columbia, and eagles. The details of these pieces are particularly well done.

these is Paul Bunyan, the mythical logger of the Great Lakes and Pacific Northwest—the man who, according to legend, created the Grand Canyon and Puget Sound—whose legendary strength and association with his blue ox, Babe, have been the stuff of both folk tales and folk art.

Figures of Bunyan are often themselves of legendary size: carvings eight to ten feet high embellish gas stations, tourist camps, and shopping centers clear across the nation. Most examples are of fairly recent vintage, and Styrofoam and plastic are beginning to take the place of natural materials. Another outsized lumberjack hero is Tony Beaver, described as a "sort of relative" of Bunyan's. Tony Beaver exists in tall tales told by southern lumberjacks; his associate is Big Henry.

By far the most prominent of these legendary characters is the colorful figure of Uncle Sam. The origin of Uncle Sam remains somewhat uncertain, but it seems most likely that his name, if not his likeness, comes from that of a Troy, New York, meat contractor named Samuel Wilson. Wilson supplied meat to the U.S. Army during the War of 1812, and the crates containing his rations were stamped "U.S." The initials stood for "United States," but Wilson's workers joked that the letters actually stood for "Uncle Sam," the nickname by which Wilson was known to his friends and workers. Somehow, this little joke spread. The earliest known use of Uncle Sam for the United States was in an editorial for the *Troy Post* for September 7, 1813. The figure's distinctive garb evolved from the imaginations of generations of political cartoonists, who have pitted Uncle Sam against other national personifications,

Fire mark bust of William Penn, painted cast iron; made for the Penn Fire Insurance Company, Pittsburgh, Pennsylvania, 1841–45. Like other advertisers, insurance firms often utilized figures of great men, hoping, no doubt, that some of the renowned man's virtues might rub off—at least in the consumer's mind—on the product or services offered.

such as England's John Bull.

Whatever his true lineage might be, Uncle Sam's position as a symbol of the indomitable American spirit remains unquestioned, and he is one of the most popular members of the folk artist's pantheon.

Perhaps the most popular form in which this figure is found is that of the whirligig. There are complex forms, such as the *Uncle Sam Rides a Bicycle*, in the collection of the Museum of American Folk Art, in which the wildly pedaling figure bears a great flag that is painted on one side with the Stars and Stripes and on the other with the Canadian emblem (reflecting, perhaps, a hope of unification or, more likely, the unknown artist's proximity to the northern border).

More often found, though, is the simple 'gig with paddle arms. These are usually embellished with stars or stripes to complement the figure's costume. Among the examples shown here is a black version, reflecting a more universal view of Uncle Sam.

Though the character, as personification of the nation, dates to Revolutionary War times—when he was known as Brother Jonathan and didn't sport a beard—carved and painted renditions of Uncle Sam are almost always of quite recent vintage. Whirligigs usually date to the late 19th or early 20th century, and most other carvings are of like age. The sculptural piece featuring Sam holding the American eagle on his outstretched arm, illustrated here, is typical. It was made by the contemporary folk carver Bryan McNutt.

In another popular form, the mailbox holder, Uncle Sam's arm supports not the national bird but an ordinary mailbox. These usually life-size, two-dimensional saw-cut figures were made in some quantity at the time of the 1976 bicentennial, but earlier examples are known.

Other somewhat unlikely guises for the popular character include those of doorstops, cardboard candy containers (such as the one shown here, which was probably designed to grace the table at a Fourth of July party), rag dolls, and the chalk figures given away as prizes at fairs and sideshows. The variations on the Uncle Sam figure seem almost without end. Some are one-of-a-kind creations; others are commercial products whose design shows the spark of individual creativity. Immediately recognizable—even when he seems to belong more directly to a carnival than the stuff of history—Uncle Sam remains one of America's most embraceable characters.

MiltonBonD
©1983

In God We Trust

For early Americans, no institution had greater significance—on a direct, personal level—than the church. The search for religious freedom brought peoples of many diverse beliefs to these shores, and this diversity has had many consequences for Americans. In America, faith has taken many forms, and these are sometimes far removed from traditional religious norms.

Academic religious art of the sort well established in Europe and Asia is practically unknown in America, but Americans have created a vast quantity of religious folk art. Indeed, one can say with some justification that all American religious art is folk art.

The many forms of American religious folk art reflect the many different faiths that took hold across the nation. Thus, the religious folk art of the Northeast, South, and Midwest owes much to the traditional sanctified art of England, while that of the Southwest mirrors the traditions of the Iberian Peninsula.

In New England, where the Puritan ethic forbade the worship of graven images, artistic expression was confined to architecture, with the stark white meetinghouse embodying the prevailing religious enthusiasm. The building of this edifice was a great event in the life of a community and was cause for celebrations much in excess of what we normally think of today as "religious." For example, when the meetinghouse at Rockingham, Vermont, was built in 1787, its master carpenter, General John Fuller, rode the main roof beam, or plate, as it was lifted into place. As was noted by a local historian:

OPPOSITE (DETAIL) AND ABOVE: *Christmas in Connecticut*, reverse-glass painting; by Milton Bond, Connecticut, 1983. This work captures the nostalgia of a traditional country Christmas, with worshipers arriving for church services, children playing in the snow, and, of course, the tree on the village green.

ABOVE: Noah's ark, painted wood with lithographed paper decoration; United States or Germany, 1850–1900. Fascination with the biblical story of the flood and the ark led to the production of many toys like this. In very religious homes, these arks were the only toys children were allowed to play with on the Sabbath (the arks were considered "instructional"). OPPOSITE TOP: Noah's ark, painted wood with lithographed paper decoration; New England or New York, ca. 1877. This unusual ark combines the boat and animals with a strip of paper mounted on rollers that can be viewed through an opening in the ark's side. Turning the rollers causes a panorama of printed animals to pass before the viewer. OPPOSITE BOTTOM: Figure of Saint Francis of Assisi, carved and painted wood; attributed to Ben Ortega, Tesuque, New Mexico, ca. 1975. Hewn from a log and embellished with a few nails and a bit of rope, this powerful work reflects the strong Hispanic tradition of the southwestern United States.

"After he got everything ready the old General took his bottle of rum in one hand, a tumbler in the other, and stood on the bent of the plate on the south side, then gave the order to put it up in that position. He rode on the plate, and he was a man weighing 200 pounds. When they had got it up, he stood on the plate, drank his health to the crowd below, then threw down his bottle and tumbler and called for the ladder, coming down amid loud and long cheering."

Faith in a hereafter was critical at a time when few survived past age fifty and parents could anticipate burying half their offspring. The women who bore these children became the chroniclers of family deaths, recording them meticulously in the mourning, or memorial, pictures and needleworks that are now regarded as among the highest forms of 19th-century American folk art.

Most mourning pictures share common motifs: a tomb, mourners, and, inevitably, a weeping willow. Such works indulged in abundant romantic sentimentality. At the time they were made, however, these pieces were not always so well respected. Harriet Beecher Stowe, in her *Oldtown Folks* (1869), described one of the many female seminaries where young ladies were taught, among other skills, the art of the memorial:

"Miss Titcomb exercised a general supervision over the manners, morals and health of the young girls connected with the institution . . . and also gave special attention to the female accomplishments. These so far as I could observe consisted largely in embroidering mourning

pieces, with a family monument in the center, a green ground worked in chenille and floss silk, with an exuberant willow-tree and a number of weeping mourners whose faces were often concealed by flowing pocket handkerchiefs."

Despite this critical evaluation, the mourning, or memorial, picture was an important artistic outlet at a time when women were, for the most part, denied access to more traditional and academic areas, such as painting in oils. Moreover, the folk artist who created such a work provided not only a bit of history—usually set forth in the names and dates inscribed on the monument—but also, through the clothing worn by the mourners pictured, some of the few remaining pictorial clues to how people dressed in the early 19th century. Also, on rare occasions, the artist would include as background an accurate rendition of an early American community. Among the known views are those of Harvard College at Cambridge, Massachusetts, and the New Haven village green. We are grateful for any such historical views from those prephotography days.

Religious dissenters and utopians of many sorts swarmed to the United States, where they could express themselves freely. They met certain limitations, of course, if not in law, then in practice, for even today religious bigotry is not unknown, especially toward those whose behavior as well as beliefs transgress accepted norms. In general, however, Americans welcomed and tolerated the practitioners of all faiths. To Europeans, this toleration was striking:

"In the religious freedom which America enjoys I see a more unquestioned superiority. In Britain we enjoy toleration, but here they enjoy liberty. . . . In America the question is not 'What is his creed?' but 'What is his conduct?' Jews have all the privileges of Christians. Episcopalians, Presbyterians and Independents meet on common ground. No religious test is required for public office . . . and in every court throughout the country, it is optional whether you give your affirmation or your oath." (John M. Duncan, *Travels Through Part of the United States and Canada, in 1818 and 1819*)

This toleration was often sorely tested by separatist groups like the Shakers and Mormons, whose customary behavior either threatened the continuation of the general society (Shaker rejection of procreation) or violated the nation's basic moral tenets (Mormon belief in polygamy).

Such cults, however, were often the source of the finest American religious folk art. The Zoarites of Ohio produced a variety of practical items, such as tinware, quilts, and furniture, often decorated with the red, blue, and yellow Zoar star. Olof Krans, painter of the Bishop Hill, Illinois, separatist society, is generally regarded as one of the most important American folk artists.

The Shakers, or the United Society of Believers in Christ's Second Appearing, as they preferred to style themselves, are probably the best known of the separatist religious groups. Established in England before 1750, the group encountered persecution, causing most members,

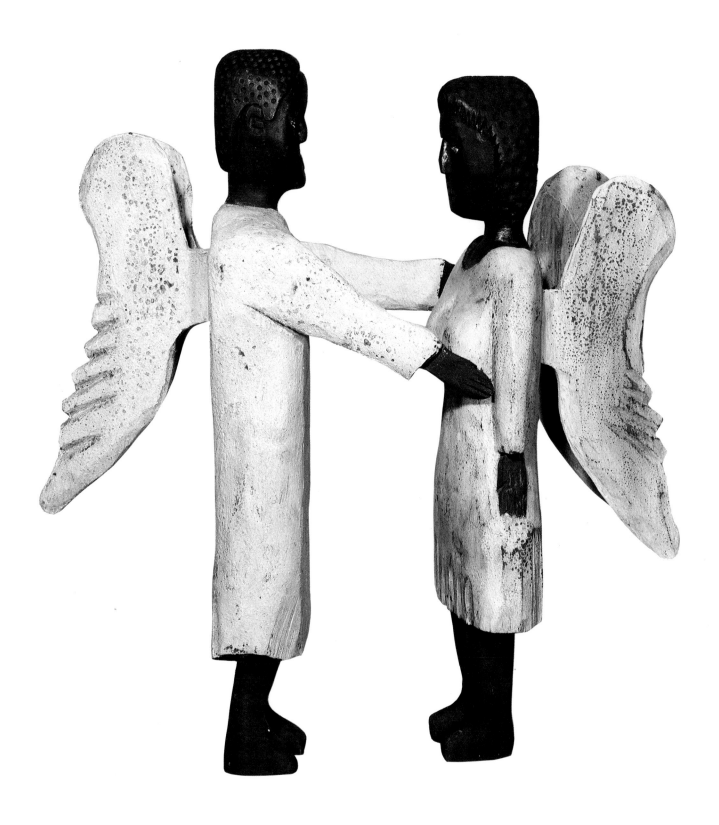

OPPOSITE TOP: Weathervane in the form of the archangel Gabriel, sheet and wrought iron; New England, 1850–75. Gabriel, God's messenger destined to sound his horn on Judgment Day, was a common weathervane form for churches and graveyards. OPPOSITE BOTTOM: Figure, carved and painted wood with metal and hair details; Mohawk Valley, New York, ca. 1910. Generally thought to represent Father Time, this piece is articulated so that the right arm can swing down to strike the bell with the sickle. ABOVE: *The Reunion*, carved and painted pine; by Stephen Huneck, Vermont, 1984. The suggestion is that of a meeting of spouses or lovers in the afterlife, a popular theme with many folk artists.

Wedding, oil on Masonite; by Malcah Zeldis, New York City, 1973. This scene of an Orthodox Jewish wedding springs directly from the artist's own background. Born in New York, she went to Israel at the age of eighteen, where she worked on collective farms and raised a family. She now lives in New York City.

Crucifixion, oil on canvas; by Peter "Charlie" Bochero, Leechburg, Pennsylvania, ca. 1960. Considered an "isolate"—one removed from the normal currents of life around him—Bochero worked in secret. His paintings, which blend religious themes with space visitors, were not discovered until after his death, in 1962.

under the leadership of one Ann Lee (later known as Mother Ann), to flee to America, where they arrived in 1774.

The sect established itself first at Niskayuna, west of Albany, New York, and then gradually spread throughout portions of New England, west to Ohio, and south to Kentucky. In the 1850s, during the height of its popularity, the Shaker faith could claim over six thousand adherents living in eighteen communities.

Economic changes and the group's ban on sex and procreation (Mother Ann considered a consummated marriage to be no less than "a covenant with death and an agreement with hell") led to a falling off in membership, until today only a few aged members remain.

Mother Ann's admonition to the faithful "Hands to work and hearts to God" reflected a philosophy of work and life that resulted in wonderful craftsmanship. Chairs, tables, baskets, boxes, dippers—whatever the pieces might be, they were created with a loving skill that today makes them highly sought after by collectors of folk art.

·Simplicity and practicality were the keynotes for this work, with the Shakers' governing code, *The Millennial Laws*, specifically enjoining the membership that "in every place, especially in large Societies, where you have considerable to vend in publick markets, that it be plain and simple, and of good and substantial quantity which becomes your calling and profession."

As practical as they were, the Shakers were capable of remarkable creativity. Their inspirational drawings produced during the 1840s

ABOVE: Inscription and design, ink on cherry log; by David W. Fox, Tarr, Pennsylvania, 1932. Nothing is known of Fox, who covered this eighteen-inch-long log with religious homilies and a drawing of a log cabin that he titled "The Dear Old Home." The obsessive nature of the piece indicates that Fox's work would fall within the category now called outsider art. FOLLOWING PAGES: *Hancock Shaker Village,* oil on canvas; by Kathy Jakobsen, New York City, 1981. This painting depicts a major Shaker settlement as it would have appeared at its height during the mid 19th century. Particularly prominent is an innovative round barn, designed to facilitate care of livestock.

ABOVE: Shaker carrier, painted ash and maple; probably from Enfield, New Hampshire, 1860–80. Handled carriers like this were used by the Shakers when gathering the herbs they grew and sold for use in cooking and for medicinal purposes. Since such pieces are usually unmarked, they may be hard to distinguish from similar ones made by non-Shaker craftsmen. OPPOSITE TOP: Shaker dipper, turned and bentwood ash and maple with a pine bottom; Enfield or Canterbury, New Hampshire, 1870–80. The simplicity and classic lines of this piece are typical of the best Shaker work. Dippers were made in nests of three sizes and were being sold to outsiders as early as 1789. OPPOSITE BOTTOM: Stack of oval Shaker boxes, maple with pine tops and bottoms and ranging in length from four to thirteen inches; New York or New England, 1870–80. Oval boxes are among the most popular of Shaker collectibles. FOLLOWING PAGES: *Amish Girls Quilting*, oil on canvas; by Janis Price, Ohio, 1980. An unworldly religious group that shuns the use of such modern innovations as automobiles and televisions, the Amish have become prosperous farmers in Pennsylvania, Ohio, and Indiana as well as in some parts of Canada.

combined artistry with a finely honed ascetic sensibility that strove always for a divine perfection.

Plainness was also the hallmark of another separatist group, the Amish of Pennsylvania, Ohio, and Indiana. Eschewing, even today, most modern conveniences, including the automobile—but wisely favoring marriage and the family—the Amish have thrived as farmers.

They have also proven creative, especially in the area of needlework; their geometric quilts have earned the respect and admiration of collectors not only here but in Europe and Asia.

Closely related to the spiritual were various secret societies, the membership of which ascribed to certain generally accepted religious tenets but embellished these with elaborate rituals. Chief among these societies is the Masons, or Freemasons; indeed, the Masons form the largest secret society in the world. The first Masonic lodge in America was founded in Philadelphia in 1730; Benjamin Franklin was a member. Many other American leaders of the Revolutionary period were Masons, including Paul Revere and John Hancock (Benedict Arnold, too, was a Mason, but his lodge expunged his name following his act of treason). George Washington became a member in 1752, and, in fact, thirteen presidents have been Masons. The Masons' elaborate rites and ceremonies utilize many symbols, including the instruments of the stonemason—the plumb, square, level, and compasses—and make reference to such apocryphal events as the building of King Solomon's Temple. These symbols and themes show up on the many decorated

folk objects associated with the Masons, such as the aprons and furniture employed in Masonic halls.

In the southwestern states, settlers of Hispanic background brought with them the tradition of the *santero*, the "painter of saints," whose role it was to carve religious statues, or *bultos*, and to paint religious icons, or *retablos*. Though largely ignored until recent years by those who presumed to define what was "American folk art," this work includes some of the earliest and finest pieces made on this continent.

Santos paintings and sculpture are based on a remembrance and transformation of Spanish academic works and reflect not only the creativity of the individual craftsman, who often had never seen an academic work, but also the introduction of native American themes and techniques.

Other streams of faith and religious experience have influenced and continue to influence American folk art. Greek Orthodox motifs appear in the work of the Maine carver John Perates; the Jewish tradition is represented in the powerful, expressionist paintings of Malcah Zeldis.

Among the works illustrated here is a small log on which David W. Fox, a folk artist and religious enthusiast of the 1930s, painstakingly blended biblical passages with memories of his youth, weaving the whole about a charming rendition of a log cabin. Though based on the Judeo-Christian tradition, such pieces reflect an extremely personal religious view.

RIGHT: *Saint Luke*, relief-carved and painted wood; by John Perates, Portland, Maine, ca. 1940. Perates was a Greek immigrant, and his work is derived from the Byzantine icons with which he was familiar. Perates donated this and other similar panels, as well as an elaborately carved pulpit, to Portland's Greek Orthodox Church. Unused for years, they were discovered in a cellar during the early 1970s. OPPOSITE TOP: *The Holy Family*, carved and painted cottonwood; by Felix A. Lopez, Espanola, New Mexico, 1979. Though a contemporary folk carver, Lopez works in a traditional style maintained among the southwestern Spanish-Americans for hundreds of years. The holy family is one of the most popular of the forms produced. OPPOSITE BOTTOM: *Nazarene Christ*, carved and painted wood, horsehair, and cloth; New Mexico, 1850–60. The style of this powerful figure is closely related to the religious carvings found in the churches of Iberia; Spanish settlers brought the style to the New World. As Spanish influence waned, local sculptors supplied the needs of isolated parishes, such as those in New Mexico.

ships with carved eagles for use as figureheads, sternboards, and gangway or cabin decorations.

His greatest triumph and arguably America's greatest eagle carving is the bird that he made for the U.S.S. *Lancaster*. This mammoth eagle has a wingspan of eighteen feet! Most of his work was much smaller, of course, and included whimsical pieces given away as gifts and sometimes embellished with appropriate greetings, such as "Merry Christmas" and "Happy Birthday."

The unquestioned reliability of the national fowl recommended it to the business community. As early as 1800, Paul Revere was using an eagle on the trade card for his cannon foundry in North Boston. Fire marks, placed by insurance companies on the buildings they insured and which, in some cases, their private fire brigades would protect, sometimes took the form of the eagle. A fire mark utilized about 1850 by the Eagle Insurance Company of Cincinnati, Ohio, depicts the eagle in a side view, crouched on a shield with his eyes fixed intently on the arrows and his back turned to the olive branch. The impression is that of an avian warrior hurtling into battle aboard some sort of spaceship: a rather unusual symbol for a firm that sold fire insurance.

Likewise, in homes, the controlled fire might be housed within a cooking or heating stove the cast-iron panels of which were embossed with representations of the same bird. The rare example illustrated here shows how far the craftsman might go in his depiction of the national symbol. The eagle, whose wings and body are oddly drag-

Foot warmer with eagle decoration, punched tin and turned pine; Northeast, 1820–50. During the first half of the 19th century, no vehicles and few public buildings were heated. Consequently, foot warmers, which could be filled with charcoal or hot coals, were widely used. Other punched decoration found on such pieces includes stars, diamonds, hearts, and flowers.

ABOVE: Crock, salt-glazed stoneware with stenciled eagle decoration; New England or New York, 1860–1900. The eagle appeared frequently as decoration on early American stoneware. In the earliest examples, the figure was scratched or incised into the clay; later it was applied in blue with a brush or slip cup; stenciling was the final method of decoration. OPPOSITE: Hooked rug, wool and cotton on burlap; New England, 1875–1900. This unusual and charming folk textile incorporates a classic eagle that appears to be hovering threateningly over several rabbits.

onlike, clutches the traditional olive branch and arrows while resting upon a stylized urn within which is a national shield. The base of the urn supports a variety of symbolic paraphernalia, including banners, liberty caps, a sword, drum, cornucopia, and scales of justice—in short, a little something for everyone.

No national, state, or local celebration was complete without the great bird, borne on a banner, hoisted aloft in papier-mâché representation, or, most transitory of all, formed in the air as the subject of a fireworks display. In describing one such event, the *Transactions of the American Institute of the City of New-York* recorded in 1852 that:

"The display was truly magnificent, brilliant in color and beautiful in design. The principal piece was composed of a central group of colossal figures . . . enclosed in an arch of arabesque work, surmounted with the American eagle . . . presenting in the whole, a front of splendid highly colored fires of ninety feet in length, by over fifty in height."

Smaller renditions of the great bird have appeared on many generations of American coins. One of the nation's first coins, a ten-dollar gold piece with an eagle stamped on the reverse side, was commonly referred to as an "eagle"; thus, the five-dollar coin became known as a "half eagle," and the twenty-dollar coin was called a "double eagle." Eagles still appear on American coins, and some recent examples, such as the Eisenhower dollar and the Susan B. Anthony dollar, picture the eagle landing on the moon.

Most of all, the nation's new symbol appeared in the home and in

Drinking flask with embossed eagle, mold-formed yellowware; Ohio, 1840–50. The form and decoration of this extremely rare example imitate the much more common glass historical flasks made during the same period. Such ceramic bottles were not as popular with drinkers as glass vessels. After all, with the glass bottles you could at least get a look at what you were drinking.

the school, where its spirited presence gave hope and offered inspiration. Women preparing textiles for home use found the eagle to be an appropriate and appealing decorative embellishment. Quilters used the regal bird as a central motif in their bed coverings, while the makers of hooked rugs might devote all or most of their surface to it.

Woven coverlets, manufactured for the most part by professional weavers, also frequently featured the bird, sometimes in combination with other patriotic icons, such as busts of Washington or nationalistic slogans like the ever-popular "Agriculture and Manufactures Are the Foundation of Our Independence."

Less often seen were samplers, textile pictures, and memorial paintings incorporating representations of eagles. In these mediums, eagles seldom dominate the composition, but might appear as minor elements, such as in borders.

Schoolmasters and the instructors in business institutes where the newly popular Spencerian script was taught used the eagle as a favorite decorative embellishment. Indeed, the bird became almost a set piece, with students proving their mastery of calligraphic penmanship by turning out a drawing complete with eagle and swirling, flowing script.

Even those who lacked any formal artistic training did not hesitate to employ their version of the national symbol. Folk artists offered oils and watercolors in which the eagle played a prominent role in historical or fanciful allegories of the American condition. Sign painters, who often had little or no formal training, utilized the great bird as the "come

on" for hotels, train stations, stage lines, and businesses of every sort.

Potters scratched the eagle into redware plates or painted it in blue slip on the surface of such mundane objects as crocks, jugs, and churns. Where they were unsure of their art, they employed stencils or used stamps that could be pressed into the soft clay, but in all cases they combined patriotic fervor with the awareness that the bird was a highly salable commodity.

This awareness was shared by glassblowers, whose whiskey flasks frequently bore a lone embossed eagle or an embossed eagle cheek by jowl with a former president or national hero. The eagle, in fact, became a standard element on these vessels. Thomas W. Dyott, a bootblack who rose to become the owner of one of Pennsylvania's major bottle factories, produced a vast number of flasks in a wide range of colors, and many of his products included an eagle. In the March 2, 1825, edition of the *Columbia Observer* he offered for sale:

"3,000 gross Washington and Eagle pint flasks, 3,000 gross Lafayette and Eagle pint flasks, 3,000 gross Dyott and Franklin pint flasks, 2,000 Ship Franklin and Agricultural pint flasks, 5,000 gross assorted Eagle pint flasks, 4,000 gross Eagle, Cornucopia and etc. half pints."

The popularity of eagle flasks reached its zenith during the period of westward expansion and rural development. Thus, the embossed eagles were frequently combined with motifs related to farming and farm production, such as flowers, morning glory vines, grapes, trees,

Historical flask with embossed eagle, mold-blown glass; Coventry, New Hampshire, 1829–32. Like many early bottles, this example is made of dark green glass, a color caused by iron impurities in the sand used in the glass mixture, or batch. The embossed eagle is of a classic form set on a field of stars.

and agricultural implements. Thanks to the folk artist's whim, eagles also appeared together with unusual motifs, such as lyres and stags.

And, in the best traditions of a democracy, the eagle was for everyone, children included. Toddlers pulled cast-iron wheel toys made in the form of eagles and equipped with tiny bells that jingled as the toy was drawn along. For older kids there were wheeled vehicles such as the kiddie car shown here. Manufactured in the early 20th century by the S. A. Smith Manufacturing Company of Brattleboro, Vermont, it is in the form of a great eagle with widespread wings. The child sat in a shield-shaped seat upon the eagle's back and supported him- or herself by gripping the wings. Who knows what fantasies of power and patriotism surged through the breasts of those youthful riders?

Though hardly a unique symbol—many nations, past and present, have adopted it as symbol—the eagle remains the motif most closely associated with the spirit and aspirations of the United States. And Americans have a valid claim to the noble bird. Many years before the Continental Congress overrode Franklin's protestations and selected the eagle for the Great Seal, the bird had done service as symbol of America. In 1734, the proprietors of the Georgia colony sent a group of Creek Indians to visit George II in England. One of the Indians, an aging chief, gave the English monarch a special gift of some eagle feathers, explaining that the feathers were a "sign of power in our land" and that they came from "the swiftest of birds . . . who flies all round our nation."

LIBERTY, THE GREAT LADY

T he great excitement surrounding the restoration of the Statue of Liberty in New York Harbor served to remind us of the important role the goddess of Liberty, symbol of democracy and the freedom offered by the nation, has played in the history of our country. Our forefathers, however, needed no such reminders, for they had long utilized the great lady in their national artistic expression.

Indeed, she antedates the establishment of the Republic. From the mid 16th century until around 1760, the newly discovered Americas were symbolized for Europeans by an Amazonian figure known as the Indian Queen, whose appearance reflected popular conceptions of Caribbean natives.

As the colonies established a feeling of independence and self-identity, the queen became a princess, England's rebellious daughter, whose dress and mien were distinctly European, as opposed to the half-clad appearance of the queen. Following the Revolution, she became a classical figure in flowing robes, associated with the symbols of freedom and victory: the liberty cap and pole, an olive branch, and, of course, the eagle.

Throughout the 19th century, this female symbol of national sovereignty appeared in many guises: as Columbia, the feminine personification of the United States; as Minerva, the mythological goddess of wisdom; or as the classical goddess of Liberty, usually wrapped in or bearing the Stars and Stripes. All this confusion came to an end with the erection, in 1886, of the Statue of Liberty. From that point on, the torch

Our Country Is Free, watercolor on paper; by Joe Miller, Illinois, ca. 1870. As did many other folk artists, Miller based his composition on a popular print, in this case a small Currier and Ives print entitled *The Star Spangled Banner*. Miller did not merely copy the lithograph, but substantially altered it in his own creative way.

and tablet replaced more militant symbols as befitting a nation grown to maturity and confidence. The statue, designed by Frédéric Auguste Bartholdi, also established Liberty's seven-spiked diadem, symbolizing the seven continents and seven seas. (The so-called Mercury dime, issued from 1916 to 1945, did cause some confusion: the coin bears a likeness of Liberty with wings on her cap, leading many Americans to mistake her for the messenger god, Mercury.)

Given Liberty's long history and her importance in the establishment and growth of our national identity, it isn't surprising that a vast amount of folk art has been based on her form. Images of Liberty range from delicate watercolors to gigantic building finials and tawdry pot-metal penny banks. Her image also appears in advertisements for generations of various products, ranging from cigars and War Bonds to painkillers and hog remedies.

Among the more impressive forms are weathervanes. The vane manufacturers A. B. and W. T. Westervelt of New York offered a flag-bearing goddess of Liberty in 1883 in sizes ranging from two to four feet. Ten years later, another maker, J. W. Fiske, was selling a similar figure but had added to his inventory the newly popular Liberty Enlightening the World, which was thirty-three inches tall and could be had for $85, a very substantial sum in those days.

The fact that citizens would pay that much for a wind-directional device reflects the enthusiasm with which the symbol of Liberty was greeted. Many of the commercially manufactured vanes were pro-

OPPOSITE: Liberty with flag and sword, carved and painted wood; New Hampshire, 1850–60. This unusually combative version of the Liberty figure once decorated a boathouse in Tufton-borough, New Hampshire. The rippling effect achieved in carving the flag is especially well done. ABOVE: Cookie box featuring the Statue of Liberty, lithographed tin; Northeast or Midwest, 1930–40. Throughout the 20th century, the Statue of Liberty has remained a popular symbol, appealing to both Americans and to foreigners, for whom it is always a required stop on any visit to "the States."

duced from the time of the 1876 centennial until the conclusion of World War I, a period of particular patriotic enthusiasm.

Not everyone could afford a factory-made weathervane, of course, and many of those who could not created their own, employing as models the several versions of Liberty available in popular publications. Homemade versions in sheet iron, tin, and wood were usually painted in bright colors, the fading of which over long periods of time has left them with an appealing patina.

Carved and painted figures of Liberty appeared as sculpture in public places and private homes and were mounted on rooftops. Public buildings such as courthouses and city halls were frequently blessed with such statues, some of which assumed truly gargantuan proportions. The cast-zinc head illustrated here is twenty inches high and once topped a figure fully ten feet tall. Placed atop a five or six story building, such a figure must have created a sense of awe when viewed from a distance.

Most of the larger Liberty figures, particularly those made of wood, have succumbed to the ravages of time. Some examples, however, can still be found. An immense Statue of Liberty, complete with electrical torch, still stands above a storage warehouse on upper Broadway in Manhattan. Other examples, often neglected, can be found along the byways of other cities as well. Such large sculpture was expensive and usually reflected either public expenditures or public display of the wealth and ambition of an individual.

For those of more modest ambitions, the form might serve as a gatepost finial, a mailbox support, or a whirligig. Finials would be either carved from a solid log with such extras as arms, flags, and torch added or would be made from many small pieces individually carved and then glued together and then mounted on the gate or over the door of the patriot's home. Smaller pieces might be shaped to serve as mantel ornaments or to be used as decorations in public buildings, lodges, or even private homes.

Few such pieces are made today, but an interesting contemporary form is the Liberty mailbox support or light post. Such examples are typically cut from plywood or three-quarter-inch pine with a jigsaw and are then painted. A metal mailbox extends from the hand. Many such pieces were produced around the time of the 1976 bicentennial, and the better ones are already being recognized as 20th-century folk art.

Whirligigs in the form of the goddess of Liberty are also popular. Few early examples have survived, but a substantial number made during the past few decades are known. A contemporary craftsman has even created one commemorating the recent restoration of the full-size statue. Tiny workmen scurry about the figure, adding authenticity to the scene.

Liberty Giving Sustenance to the Eagle, oil on canvas in an oval frame; Georgia or Florida, early 19th century. Various versions of this scene are known, and Liberty in several guises (as the goddess of youth or justice, for example) is closely associated with the eagle, who may hover above her or repose on her arm.

Journey's End, oil on canvas; by Malcah Zeldis, New York City, 1985. This touching painting portrays the excitement, anxiety, and hope of immigrants who have at last reached the promised land beneath the sheltering arms of the great statue. As one who lived away from her native land for many years, Zeldis brought a particular personal poignancy to this work.

Needlework picture, silk and satin; East or Midwest, ca. 1900. This patriotic piece was made from a pattern and is similar in composition to the crazy quilts produced in great quantity at the turn of the century.

And the lady has gone to sea as a popular subject for figureheads and other ship carvings. Female figures had always been popular ornaments for sailing ships, so it was quite understandable that the seamen of the new nation adopted Liberty as their guide through stormy and sometimes hostile seas. Though particularly popular as a decoration for warships, the figure might be found on anything from a clipper ship to a pilot boat.

Liberty also often appeared among the motifs utilized by scrimshanders, sailors who decorated whalebone and other ivory with carved and incised work. From the early 1800s until the turn of this century, sailors spent much of their spare time creating scrimshaw. Patriotic themes were among those most often inscribed on the whalebone, and Liberty in one of her various guises was a popular decorative device.

In most cases, the figure of Liberty would be copied from a popular print or magazine by the simple expedient of soaking the paper until it was soft, laying it on the bone, and then picking out the outline with a pin. The pinpricks would then be joined and the resultant border filled in with ink or lampblack. Sometimes, the figures were also tinted with watercolors or dyes.

Fine old scrimshaw is among the most sought after of American antiques. Unfortunately, this popularity has led to frequent reproduction, and would-be collectors should use great caution in purchasing examples.

Head of Liberty sculptural fragment, zinc; Pennsylvania, ca. 1876. This is a remnant of the kind of large neoclassical figures made for public buildings during the 19th century. Over the course of time, most such figures have vanished, along with the structures they once embellished.

Although Americans revered the figure of Liberty, they did not hesitate to modify and adapt her as they pleased. Nearly every town had its Liberty Belle tavern, the dooryard of which might be adorned with a swinging sign featuring a painted or carved variation of the great lady. When political marchers went forth in torchlight parades, they bore before them, as proof of the righteousness of their cause, painted oilcloth banners on which she appeared, and on their heads they wore top hats adorned with her image. And when, exhausted by their labors, they paused for a swig of whiskey, they were likely to take it from a flask embossed with the lady's head.

Most homes and public halls were decorated with folk paintings of Liberty, and the fire engines dragged through the streets to the scene of the most recent conflagration were also embellished with her image, as were the leather buckets passed from hand to hand by the fire brigade.

Folk renditions of the Liberty figure vary greatly, reflecting not only changes in the public apprehension of the figure but also the skills and preferences of individual artists.

The great lady made some of her earliest appearances in watercolor and textile mourning pictures, in which she might be found drooping with sorrow at the grave of Washington, usually in company with one or more Revolutionary War veterans. Oils included parlor works, like the one shown here in which Liberty is seen offering sustenance to the great eagle of the Republic. (Liberty often appears together with the national bird, and pictures of her giving the eagle a

utilitarian storage function of which was belied by the bright cobalt-blue floral patterns, birds, and other whimsical designs and creatures with which they were decorated. Even farm implements were often carved and decorated in order that a bit of beauty of whimsy might relieve some of the tedium of long days in the fields.

Children, the center of the household, played as they do today with toys that taught them home tasks and helped smooth the transition to adulthood. The dollhouse illustrated here, for example, is a miniature replica of the sort of dwelling common in the late 1800s, and the remarkable chrome-and-enamel stove is an almost exact duplicate of the coal range on which its young owner's mother prepared the family meals. Perhaps the most unusual is the child's sewing machine that is itself in the form of a woman sewing at a full-size version. Like other pieces of folk art, toys were made with both skill and a sense of beauty.

Man on a bicycle, painted tin, wood, and iron; New York, 19th century. This whimsical figure is dated 1839 but is believed to have been made somewhat later. By the end of the 1800s, bicycles were common in the United States, with riders often organized into clubs for day trips and competitions.

TOP: Construction toy, the "District School," saw-cut and painted wood; Charles M. Crandall Company, Montrose, Pennsylvania, 1870–80. Playing school was a popular pastime, especially for preschool children, and this easily assembled set was quite popular in its day. Its charming folk quality makes it a current collector's favorite. ABOVE: Document or storage box, painted tin with brass hardware; New York or New England, 1830–50. Known as toleware, hand-painted tin utensils offered a wide and challenging field for the folk painter. While flowers were the most popular subject matter, birds, animals, and occasionally human figures can also be found.

All of this was needed, for the rural home was often a harsh and primitive abode, as may be seen from the following description dictated by an early settler and printed in *History of Coshocton County, Ohio: Its Past and Present* (1881):

"The furniture of the backwoods matched the architecture well. There were a few quaint specimens of cabinet work dragged into the wilderness, but these were sporadic and not common . . . on great occasions, when an extension table was needed, the door was lifted off its hinges . . . a large tea chest, cut in two and hung by strings in the corners with the hollow side outward, constituted the bookcases and the rest [of the furniture] was hewn and whittled out according to the fashion of the times, to serve their day and be supplanted by others as the civilization of the country advanced."

Today, surviving examples of such furnishings are regarded as among the most appealing of folk art. This is particularly true of those pieces that were designed initially to be things of beauty, such as the gifts traditionally given at the tin and wooden wedding anniversaries. In his *Wedding Etiquette and Usages of Polite Society* (1880), George D. Carroll described some such objects:

"Mr. and Mrs. T. Chesley Richardson . . . celebrated their 'wooden wedding' on Tuesday evening, January 27. Many unique and appropriate presents were received. Cedar tubs and bowls, and pails . . . elaborately carved tables with embroidered coverings . . . wall brackets of artistic design . . . paintings on wood . . . beautifully worked wooden plaques, boxes of beautiful woods for various uses, etc. etc."

Occupying the true place of honor in every home that could afford them were family portraits: folk representations of mother,

father, and, particularly, the offspring. Children were often depicted with their pets and small toys.

Every parent hoped for children who would grow up healthy and, through the opportunities offered by this most generous of countries, achieve goals never dreamed of by prior generations. One of the paths to such success was universal public education. Europeans marveled at the American dedication to "book learning." Anthony Trollope remarked:

"I do not remember that I ever examined the rooms of an American without finding books or magazines in them. . . . Men and women of the classes . . . who earn their bread by the labour of their hands . . . talk of reading and writing as of arts belonging to them as a matter of course, quite as much as the arts of eating and drinking. . . . A porter or a farmer's servant in the States is not proud of reading and

ABOVE: *Why Work?* painted relief-carved wood; by William Ned Cartledge, Atlanta, Georgia, 1980. Unlike most folk artists, Cartledge expresses his political and social beliefs in his work. FOLLOWING PAGES: *The Game*, fresco on masonry; by Janet Munro, New York, 1984. Munro has captured perfectly the idealized tranquility of the home. Cats sit about the floor, while two generations partake of a slow-paced game of checkers. With humor typical of the folk artist, Munro has added to the walls two of her own miniature landscapes.

Watercolor on paper; New England, 1800–20. This scene of a young woman before a seminary or boarding school was probably done by a student. Seminaries offered young women an opportunity for education at a time when few women had access to other schools.

writing. It is to him quite a matter of course." (Anthony Trollope, *North America*, 1862)

Basic to the concept of universal public education was the one-room schoolhouse, the doors of which were open to all, without cost or discrimination. This ideal was not always realized, of course, particularly during the early years of the Republic. Until well into the 1800s, private academies or female seminaries provided an education, at cost, for the well-to-do. Those less fortunate could educate their children only if their community could afford to build a schoolhouse and employ a teacher. Nor were these schools exactly comparable to our modern ones. Rural schools often met for only a brief period of the year so that the children could be free to work with the rest of the family during the important planting and harvesting periods. Because of such absences, the scholars were frequently too old for their grade levels, and it was not uncommon for an instructor in his or her early twenties to be teaching students only a few years younger. Small wonder that most rural districts preferred male teachers, the stronger the better!

Both private and public education have left a legacy of folk art. From the private seminaries come samplers, mourning pictures, and theorems, some of which, like the watercolor illustrated here, included among their motifs representations of the academies attended by the young women who created them. Samplers sometimes bear the name of the school where they were made, as in the well-known samplers made at Westtown, a Friends school near Philadelphia.

From the public schools come what are perhaps the best known school-related textiles, the traditional schoolhouse quilts, the patterns of which consist of the repetition of a single motif—the one-room schoolhouse. Though the schoolhouse may vary in design, having one or two chimneys or perhaps being embellished with a bell tower, the schoolhouse quilt remains consistent both in its pattern and in its universal appeal to quilt lovers. No doubt this appeal is due, at least in part, to that fact that even today there are many Americans who obtained at least a portion of their education in such a structure.

Given the importance of education, it is suprising that so few early folk paintings of schools exist. Perhaps the young scholars, like their present-day peers, had no wish to be reminded of a learning process that, while important, could also be tedious. Quite a few contemporary folk artists, however, have taken their schooldays as subject matter, depicting not only the traditional rural cabin but also later and larger city schools.

The educational process served another purpose, for it was in rural schools that many children were first introduced to watercolor, sandpaper and charcoal painting, and the other artistic techniques that they later utilized in creating folk art.

Windmill weight in the form of a rooster, painted cast iron; Elgin Windmill Power Company, Elgin, Illinois, 1880–1910. Designed to balance the vanes of a windmill, these weights occupied a prominent spot on the farm horizon. They were often cast in the shape of domestic animals—cows, bulls, horses, and fowl.

brightened the kitchen and pantry with crocks, the surfaces of which were covered with bunches of flowers—a great blessing, especially in northern regions where little in the way of greenery was evident six months out of each year.

Other pieces were embellished with birds, some of which—such as the chicken pecking corn in the dooryard—were immediately recognizable to the rural householder. Others of a more fanciful nature were, perhaps, designed to provide an amusing topic of conversation for their owners. The lions and elephants found on a few rare containers certainly must have served that purpose. In any case, the potter contributed an often overlooked element to the rural folk scene.

Also found in the kitchen were butter molds and cake molds, many of which were carved by hand. The designs of these utilitarian objects are often based on national symbols: popular designs for butter molds include sheaves of wheat, hearts, and stars; cake molds were sometimes made in eagle patterns. Indeed, cake molds were frequently made to commemorate important national events—one example bears the inscription "York Town 1781," and another, made to celebrate Lafayette's visit to this country in 1824, shows the beloved Frenchman together with an eagle and overflowing cornucopias.

Although only a few quilts are based on specifically rural settings, such scenes are often the central composition element in late-19th- and early 20th-century hooked rugs. Some of these floor coverings focus on a traditional scene—farmhouse, barns, and livestock—while others

Bank in the form of a rooster, painted cast iron; Hubley Manufacturing Company, Lancaster, Pennsylvania, 1920–25. Thrift was and still is a rule of farm life. Perhaps the suggestion offered the young saver by this bank's form was that through collecting pennies, a few chickens might be purchased.

Hooked rug, wool, felt, and cotton on burlap; by Ethel Bishop, Maine, 1979. For a rural rug maker, bulls would have been a common sight. Other farm animals frequently appearing on hooked rugs are horses, sheep, pigs, and such fowl as hens, roosters, and pigeons.

feature domestic fowl, cows, or horses.

The charm of these rugs is derived not only from the subject matter but from the manner in which the pieces were constructed. While some were hooked over preprinted patterns, many others were individual creations in which the farm wife immortalized a cow, chicken, horse, or place with which she was familiar.

Elizabeth Waugh, in her *Collecting Hooked Rugs*, describes one instance in which this process went somewhat awry. When visiting a rug maker on the isolated Newfoundland shore, she chanced upon an unusual-looking piece, the central design of which resembled an octopus or squid. Intrigued, she asked what it was supposed to represent.

"A ram," replied the rug's creator, using the local term for tomcat. When the astounded visitor remarked that she had never seen a cat with so many legs, her hostess explained, "Didn't have no pictures of a ram, [so] us first catched the ram; then us held him down on the mat and us drawed around him. He kicked somewhat . . ."

Some of the most charming farm-related objects are the folk toys played with yesterday and today by children both in the country and in the city. Indeed, such playthings frequently offer city children their only glimpse of rural life.

Earliest in origin and most traditional are carved and painted animals and farm scenes. Complete farms including houses, barns, and outbuildings with associated livestock, a farm family, and appropriate

equipment were sold by toy dealers throughout the 19th and early 20th centuries. Greater realism and detail were sometimes added by covering the wood with lithographed paper.

Other farm-associated playthings include the familiar string toy with which a pull on the cord causes one or more jointed chickens mounted atop a wooden paddle to peck away at imaginary corn.

In the late 1800s, wonderfully detailed representations of farm vehicles and equipment began to appear. These duplicates of full-sized machinery—from the earliest horse-drawn examples to later gasoline-powered vehicles—allowed the young farmer and his urban counterpart to harvest the grains and fruits of the great plains while remaining safely at home in the yard or on the living-room rug. And thrift was encouraged in these future farmers by penny banks in the shape of such familiar animals as the cow, the horse, the pig, and the chicken. Who, having seen any of these animals eat, could doubt their storage capacity as banks?

Today, even though traditional farms, techniques, and farm life are threatened by myriad social and economic problems, rural life continues to exert a great pull on American society. While the "back to the land" movement of the late 1960s and early 1970s has largely abated in the face of both practical problems and changing life-styles, many Americans renew their heritage through the folk objects produced in the hinterland.

ABOVE: Table cover, woolen felt with appliquéd and stitched decoration; New England or Pennsylvania, 1890–1900. Though similar in appearance to quilts, these pieces were used as throws for furniture or as small rugs. Sheep and cows were popular motifs among farm wives. FOLLOWING PAGES: *Watermelon Party*, oil on canvas; by Mattie Lou O'Kelley, Georgia, 1975. Born and raised on a Georgia farm, O'Kelley is the best-known of the contemporary "memory painters," folk artists who recreate on canvas experiences remembered from their youth. Here she recalls a traditional summer social event.

DOWN TO THE
SEA IN SHIPS

S ince the end of the 18th century, the United States has been one of the world's great maritime powers, and from this attachment to the sea has flowed an immense body of folk art. The earliest works—oils, watercolors, and reverse-glass paintings—are concerned almost exclusively with nautical conflict and detail the exploits of American men and ships during the Revolutionary War and the War of 1812.

The victories won by colonial sailors astounded the world, and such captains as John Paul Jones became legends in their own time. The old sea chantey known as "The Yankee Man-of-War" dramatically depicts an encounter in 1777 between Jones's ship, the *Ranger*, and an English frigate:

"Out booms! Out booms! our Skipper cried
Out booms and give her sheet
For the swiftest keel that ever was
launched in all the British fleet
Came thundering down upon us with the
white foam at her bow . . .
But a swifter keel was 'neath our feet
nor did our sea boys dread
When the Star-spangled banner was hoisted;
to the mizzen peak was spread,
And amid a thundering shower of shot
with stunsails hoisting away

Mariner's compass pattern quilt, pieced cotton with appliqué design; Virginia, ca. 1900. Except for those in the well-known mariner's compass pattern, quilts with a nautical motif are fairly uncommon. This example combines customary motifs, such as the chain and anchor, with the hourglass, a reminder, perhaps, of how short a sailor's life could be.

Down the North Channel

Paul Jones did steer just at the break of day."

The second conflict, the War of 1812, was fought largely to protect American sailing rights, as is evidenced from the following lines from the forecastle song "Ye Parliament of England":

"You first confined our commerce, and said our ships shan't trade,

You next impressed our seamen, and used them as your slaves."

American warships such as the *Bon Homme Richard*, the *Wasp*, the *Enterprise*, the *Ranger*, and the *Constitution* ("Old Ironsides") gained fame in these conflicts and were assured immortality of another sort by the number of scale models made of them. Most of these models were of carved and painted wood, but some were made of bone, the so-called prisoner-of-war work produced by skilled artisans working with soup bones.

Once peace was restored, American merchantmen came to the fore. They pioneered the trade with China, opened Japan to the West, and developed the clipper ship, which revolutionized sea travel. As Lincoln Colcord noted in his introduction to *Songs of the American Sailormen* (1938):

"For a term of years, until other nations had learned to copy our designs, the American clipper sailed the seas without a rival, a supreme blend of beauty and utility, fulfilling the mind's desire for power and the heart's romantic and passionate aspiration to a degree perhaps never before attained by the efforts of man."

OPPOSITE TOP: Toy warship, saw-cut and painted wood and cardboard with lithographed paper decoration; R. Bliss Manufacturing Company, Pawtucket, Rhode Island, ca. 1895. Ships similar to this took part in the great American naval victory at Manila Bay, in 1898. OPPOSITE BOTTOM: Toy sailing ship, saw-cut and painted wood with lithographed paper decoration; W. S. Reed Toy Company, Leominster, Massachusetts, patented 1877. The great merchant ships that sailed from American ports were duplicated in miniature versions made of wood, tin, and even cast iron. This vessel is appropriately named "America." ABOVE: Clockwork-powered toy steamboat, the "Puritan," painted cast iron with brass and steel; Wilkins Toy Company, Keene, New Hampshire, 1890–1900. Wind-up cast-iron toys are rare, probably because it was difficult for the mechanism to propel such heavy objects—tin toys were much more suitable.

Cape Cod Harbor, oil on board; New England, 1890–1900. The unknown folk artist who created this work caught the sense of a windy day on the coast with ships under way and flags flying from the taller buildings.

The building and sailing of the great merchantmen captured the imagination of public and artist alike, and even today, with many faster means of transportation, the allure remains. Kathy Jakobsen, for example, frequently turns to this subject. Her *Ship Building*, shown here, illustrates the role of the many small New England shipyards in the process by which pine logs from the forests of Maine and New Hampshire were converted into the world's fastest sailing vessels.

The end product is seen in the reverse-glass painting of the clipper ship *Sarah* of Portland, Maine, which was executed in China around 1850. By that time, American merchantmen were filling their hulls in the eastern ports, and local artists were filling the Yankee sailors' orders for paintings to be taken home as souvenirs. Though not produced by American folk artists, such port, or "Hong," paintings are among the most sought after of nautical works.

The time of the great ships passed, but even at the turn of the century, when they were being replaced by side-wheelers and steamers, they could still command respect. The unidentified artist who created the port scene shown here captured this transition well. In the foreground are two traditional sailing vessels, but in the background, hovering against the horizon like a bird of ill omen, is a transitional sail-steamer.

The later steam vessels were fascinating in their own right and made their way into the nation's folk art. The side-wheelers that plied the Mississippi created legends with their great wheels and stacks and tumultuous races that lasted for miles and days and were as apt to end in fire or collision as in decisive victory. The side-wheel steamers shown here are probably navigating the Hudson River, whose high cliffs witnessed the first ship of their kind, Fulton's steamboat, launched in the early 1800s.

Some of what we now consider nautical folk art was actually a by-product of the manufacture of sailing vessels. Half-models, some as long as six feet, were used in construction and to give prospective owners an idea of the ship's lines. Unfortunately, most of the earlier examples of such models were destroyed once the vessel was completed. As a result, most half-models found today are of sporting craft made during the late 19th and 20th centuries.

Much elaborate carving and rich painting went into the creation of ship figureheads, the sculptural forms attached to the prow of sailing vessels. Figureheads were more than mere decoration; sailors developed strong emotional bonds with the ships they sailed in, and the figurehead became the symbol of the ship. Like the men of other seafaring nations, American sailors favored female figureheads. After all, ships are referred to as though they were female, and a ship's female figurehead might symbolize, for each sailorman aboard, the woman to

OPPOSITE: Figurehead, carved and painted pine; Boston, Massachusetts, or Portland, Maine, 1830–50. Women were a favorite figurehead form, reflecting, perhaps, the longing for wives and sweethearts inevitable on cruises that often lasted several years and not infrequently ended in disaster. ABOVE: *The Sinking of the Titanic*, reverse-glass painting; New York City area, 1912–15. The sinking of the great passenger ship in April 1912 led to a veritable spate of dramatic folk paintings, among which are this and a related picture in which the ship is viewed head-on.

ABOVE: Ship in a bottle, carved and painted wood; New England, late 19th century. Great puzzles to some people, these pieces were assembled within the bottle through use of folding masts and long tools. Such folk art was produced not only by sailors but by landlubbers, too. OPPOSITE: *Unidentified Sea Captain*, oil on canvas; attributed to Sturtevant J. Hamblen, Maine, 1830–50. In many 19th-century folk portraits, the trade or profession of the sitter is indicated by some object held or, perhaps, visible through a window; this man's career is clear from the rigging behind him and the telescope in his hand.

whom he hoped to safely return. Thus, Liberty and Columbia—along with a host of anonymous but usually buxom and long-haired women—were always favorites with American sailors. The figurehead shown here features a young lady clutching a bunch of roses just as she might while waiting on the dock for her sailor to return. Such figureheads no doubt served as an inspiration to the lonely sailors on ocean voyages that might last as long as three years.

Females were not the only subjects of figureheads, however. The strong patriotism of the nation's mariners made presidents and other statesmen, Indians, and characters drawn from literature and history common figurehead forms. Eagles were particularly popular; perhaps the most famous American figurehead is the enormous eagle carved in 1875 for the U.S.S. *Lancaster* by John H. Bellamy. (Patriotism was sometimes overruled by vanity or a more simple kind of loyalty: many figureheads were portraits of the ship's owner.)

Few figureheads were carved from a single piece of wood; most, in fact, were constructed from several blocks of wood doweled together. For added strength, the carving usually followed the grain of the wood. Arms were usually attached separately, and in some cases, to avoid possible damage in high seas, these appendages were detachable: the limb could be removed when the ship left port, or before an impending storm, and then reattached when the ship entered a harbor. For this reason, many surviving figureheads are missing body parts. (The resemblance of some figureheads to cigar-store Indians is not

Ship Building, oil on canvas; by Kathy Jakobsen, New York City, 1979. Many small shipyards were scattered along the New England coast from Connecticut to Maine, and until late in the 19th century, most American sailing vessels were made in that region.

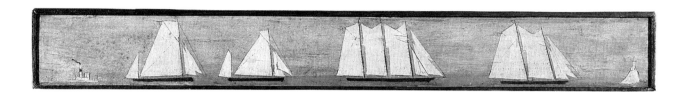

accidental: many carvers made both forms, and with the decline of the sailing ships, many former carvers of figureheads turned their skills to the tobacco trade.)

Other carved and painted portions of the ship included sternboards—on which the name of the ship might appear along with an eagle or other national symbol—and the gingerbread work that often decorated the gangway and hull. Ironwork, too, could be quite ornate.

Most nautical folk art was either produced by sailors or was produced to be sold to sailors. Best known, of course, is scrimshaw, carved and scratch-decorated pieces of ivory or other bone. Though normally associated with American whalers from the early 1800s until the end of the century, scrimshaw was produced by the sailors of many nations and was also made by nonsailors. The forms vary greatly. Teeth were decorated with incised figures, and bone was carved into such intricate shapes as clothespins, wool swifts, walking sticks, napkin rings, boxes, rolling pins, toys, pie-crust crimpers, hooks, baskets, and even birdcages. The scratch-decorated panbone (whalebone) corset stays, or "busks," shown here are particularly interesting. Incised with flowers and sailing ships, they were designed as gifts for a female favorite at a time when women compressed their figures into an hourglass shape with canvas, metal, and leather corsets. However, since they were thought of (rightly) as folk art and not something utilitarian, scrimshaw busks were seldom used. What's more, their intimate nature made them unsuitable for public display, so they were treated as personal keepsakes.

Sailor's valentines—boxed shells arranged in various patterns

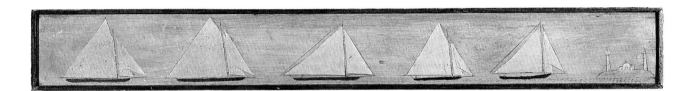

such as hearts, stars, or flowers—weren't actually made by sailors but were given by sailors as gifts. Most such novelties came from the southern climes, where a greater and more colorful variety of shells was to be found.

In their spare time, both at sea and ashore, sailors also made shadowbox pictures featuring a fully rigged half-model mounted against a painted seascape and set into a two- to four-inch-deep frame. The one shown here dates to the turn of the century and is especially appealing with its American flag and the exuberant cloud background. Modern collectors are particularly partial to such examples.

Sailors also created the mysterious ship in the bottle, achieving the seemingly impossible feat of placing a fully rigged miniature vessel inside a bottle the neck of which was clearly too small to receive it.

Special tools, collapsible sails, and various other devices made possible the miracle of the ship in the bottle, and some seamen were able to earn a small income selling these as novelties in seaports. Most examples found today were made for sale during this century. The ship illustrated here, however, dates to the 1800s, as may be ascertained from its construction and from the early hand-blown bottle in which it is placed.

The ships displayed in bottles underwent a transition parallel to the transition evident in paintings of ships, with earlier bottled ships having sails, and later examples being the steamers with which we are more familiar.

Toy ships are particularly appealing. Made of tin, wood (often covered with lithographed colored paper), or cast iron, they frequently mimicked the full-size vessels to be seen in the nation's harbors or the

Two panels depicting sailing ships against a background of land and lighthouse, oil on wood; New England, 1880–1910. It is hard to determine just what these appealing nautical paintings were used for. They may have formed part of the paneling of a room or were, perhaps, used as a trade sign.

Side-wheel steamers on the Hudson River near West Point, New York, charcoal on paper; United States, 1870–80. Such works are known as sandpaper paintings and were done on paper covered with glue and finely ground marble. These dark gray works are not in favor with most collectors, but examples like this can be charming.

Mourning picture made to commemorate the death of Admiral Oliver H. Perry, charcoal on paper; New England, ca. 1819. As a great American naval hero—the victor at Lake Erie—Perry was honored in many ways, not the least of which was this touching memorial.

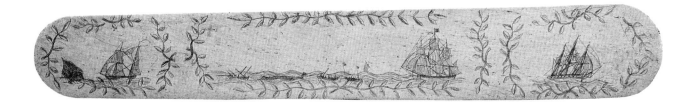

ships, such as the *Constitution*, that had played a role in our country's history. Among the examples shown here are an American warship on wheels and a cast-iron side-wheeler.

Sailing ships also appeared on stoneware jugs and crocks, incised into the soft clay or, later, painted on in cobalt blue. For those who could afford the finer white earthenware, there were transfer-decorated tea sets extolling the triumphs of Admiral Dewey at Manila Bay. Of course, such items were seldom made by sailors, but they were often sold to them or to their wives or to the countless other Americans who have been a part of this nation's great seafaring tradition.

There were also textile pictures of ships. Some of these were made by women, but certain commercial examples were made by men. Other nautical items made to be sold included the many wonderful ship models made for sale to tourists in seafaring towns like Salem and Portland and the unusual, early 20th-century reverse-glass paintings that feature such historic maritime events as the sinking of the *Titanic*.

Women whiled away the lonesome hours until their seafarers might return creating various textiles with nautical themes. Quilts might have an overall sail or ship motif; hooked rugs might feature a ship under full sails, often passing a lighthouse—a symbol, perhaps, of the long-awaited return to home port, a homecoming made poignant in a traditional American sea chantey:

"Rolling home, rolling home
Rolling home across the sea
Rolling home, dear land, to thee"

OPPOSITE: Pair of busks, panbone (a type of whalebone) with scrimshaw decoration; New England, 1830–60. Busks were used to stiffen 19th-century corsets and were an intimate gift. The incised sailing ships on these pieces are typical of the work done by American sailors. ABOVE: Sailing ship shadowbox, carved and painted wood with paper sails and string rigging; New England, 1890–1900. The shadowbox technique, in which a half-model is set under glass within a deep frame, was frequently employed for sailor's art. Like this one, most ships so handled were accurately depicted.

The clipper ship *Sarah* off the coast at Flushing, New York, reverse-painting on glass; probably made in China for the American market, 1849. As American sailors and whalers spread throughout the Far East, they often commissioned local artists to paint pictures of their ships, and such works form an important part of American marine painting.

CELEBRATING AMERICA

Duringg the 19th century, American social life revolved around holidays and celebrations. Some of these special occasions were religious, and some were related to family events, but the majority were patriotic. By far the most important of these patriotic celebrations was the Fourth of July. Every community had its Independence Day celebration, complete with speeches by local dignitaries, parades, festive meals, and, of course, a fireworks display. The following account, from the *Hempstead Inquirer* of July 8, 1835, describes the usual goings-on, including a few instances of the misadventures attendant upon fireworks displays:

"After the exercises in the church the procession formed again and proceeded to the inn of Mr. Valentine Smith where . . . an excellent dinner was provided by Mr. Smith. The patriotic toasts of the day exhibited heartfelt bursts of feeling and the general disposition manifested was that of cordial feeling and genuine good will.

"The only incident which interfered in the least with the general manifestations of pleasure was the danger to the building of Mr. Smith . . . from a fire communicated by a large double headed cracker thrown upon it by a careless boy. The explosion raised a blaze on the shingles but it was speedily extinguished by a friendly hand.

"The entertainments of the day were concluded by a brilliant display of fireworks. . . . The revolving wheels, Roman candles, &., provided a brilliant, and to many of the spectators, rare spectacle. And, 'all went as merry as a carriage bell' with the exception of a couple of

Fourth of July on the River, acrylic on canvas; by Susan Slyman, New York, 1985. The river is the Hudson, near Slyman's home.

Statue of Liberty, 1986, reverse-glass painting; by Milton Bond, Connecticut, 1985. One of the few contemporary artists to work in this medium, Bond here captures the spectacular fireworks display and the gathering of sailing vessels that commemorated the centennial celebration of the Statue of Liberty.

Fourth of July candy boxes or party favors, lithographed paper, cardboard, and wood; United States, 1900–30. Though dangerous and the cause of many injuries, firecrackers remain a tradition of the "glorious Fourth." These candy boxes provided a safer alternative.

the wheels which thought fit to tumble from their stands and expend themselves beneath the feet of the boys."

Such exhibitions provided lively subject matter for folk artists. Paintings of parades, speechmaking, and, especially, fireworks displays form an important part of the American folk genre. The example illustrated here, by the contemporary folk painter Susan Slyman, captures well the feeling of the holiday.

Also of interest are the items created to be used during the festivities, such as costumes, decorated drums and other musical instruments, and the hats and marching staffs carried in the processions. Since most of these items were relatively fragile, few have survived the passage of the years, and because they are no longer in general use, certain examples may not be recognized. This is particularly true of the candle or kerosene lamps that were mounted on long, brightly painted poles. Used in great numbers to light the marchers' route, they are seldom seen today.

Charming post cards were created to celebrate this and similar occasions. And the many parties held on the "glorious Fourth" have spawned a fascinating array of American collectibles, including favors, napkins, candleholders, hats, and elaborate centerpieces for the table. Illustrated here is a selection of small candy boxes designed in the form of firecrackers.

While the Fourth of July was by far the most extravagant of the national patriotic celebrations, there were others, many of which

remain important today. Washington's and Lincoln's birthdays were celebrated as holidays. Family or community groups would meet for dinner, and someone would rise to read an appropriate document, such as the Declaration of Independence, Washington's Farewell Address, or the Emancipation Proclamation. Bored children were kept quiet during this period by gifts of candy, which came in novel containers, such as the hatchet and cherry-tree stump—leftovers from a celebration of Washington's birthday—illustrated here.

Flag Day brought forth a display of federal colors, while May Day, once a pagan celebration of the rites of spring, became a symbol of solidarity among the working class after the Haymarket Square riot.

Perhaps the most popular traditional American holiday is Thanksgiving. Scholars point out that harvest festivals like Thanksgiving date back to ancient times, but the American holiday dates to the day of thanks ordered by Governor William Bradford of the Plymouth Colony in 1621. Sarah Josepha Hale, editor and author (among her works is the well-known nursery rhyme "Mary Had a Little Lamb"), led a crusade to make Thanksgiving Day a nationwide celebration, and her campaign eventually led to President Lincoln's proclaiming a national Thanksgiving Day in 1863.

During the 1800s, as today, the focus of Thanksgiving was on the meal, and this was often a lavish one, as may be seen from this 1827 account given by Ms. Hale in her *Northwood, or Life North and South*:

"And now for our Thanksgiving dinner. . . . The roasted turkey

Party favors for Washington's birthday, ribbon, cardboard, and lithographed paper; United States, 1900–30. The hatchet is simply a souvenir, but the top of the stump can be removed to reveal a store of sugar candies. Mementoes of presidential birthdays are becoming harder to find as the celebrations of such events are treated with less gusto.

Untitled patriotic panel, stitching on fabric; by Thalia Nicklas, United States, 1931. A powerful folk work embodying portraits of the two greatest American presidents, this piece reflects the intense patriotism of immigrant Americans. The two snuggling spectators are Uncle Sam and Liberty.

St. Patrick's Day, oil on canvas; by Helen Fabri Smagorinsky, New York, 1984. As with many other ethnic groups, the Irish have chosen a day of national celebration during which they affirm their background while honoring their adopted nation.

Saint Patrick's Day candy containers, lithographed paper, cardboard, and tinsel with clay pipe and wire-and-thread shamrock; United States, 1920–35. The bottle at left is stoppered with a real cork, although it would not hold water (or whiskey). Traditional Irish motifs are incorporated into these novelty items.

took precedence on this occasion being placed at the head of the table . . . at the foot of the board, a sirloin of beef, flanked on either side by a leg of pork and loin of mutton, seemed placed as a bastion to defend innumerable bowls of gravy and plates of vegetables disposed in that quarter. A goose and a pair of ducklings occupied side stations on the table; the middle being graced, as it always is, on such occasions, by that rich burgomaster of the provisions, called a chicken pie."

Thanksgiving celebrations have long been a favored subject with folk artists. The 20th-century folk painter Mattie Lou O'Kelley captures the spirit of the occasion in her painting *Thanksgiving* illustrated here. A large country kitchen, complete with cast-iron coal range, accommodates both the preparation and consumption of the festive meal, with hordes of friends and relatives sitting down to dine at a long communal table. While changes in the living and work habits of many Americans have made this sort of gathering less common than it once was, there is little doubt that for most of us it is the ideal—and its mood can be duplicated by smaller groups in cramped city apartments.

The Thanksgiving meal was often accompanied by favors and novelties made especially for the event. The table might be lit by candles molded in the shape of Pilgrims or Indians, while each place setting would be graced by a brightly printed napkin with an appropriate scene and a papier-mâché candy container in the shape of a turkey.

Not all patriotic celebrations are national in scope. Many communities held—and in some cases still hold—local events commemorating

dates in their own histories. Such are Patriots' Day, celebrated in Boston and Maine, Seward's Day, celebrated in Alaska, Battle of New Orleans Day in Louisiana, the Confederate Memorial Day, and the various festivities that mark the anniversaries of the founding of a town, county, or state. Such local holidays are often occasions for self-congratulation and involve long-winded speakers who extol the virtues of the assembled citizens and note how far the community has come from its origins in forest or desert:

"There is certainly abundance of reason for rejoicing and making merry on our two-hundredth anniversary. While we may not have accomplished all that is desirable and worth working for . . . there is sufficient now completed to justify the generations that have lived and worked and passed away, in that they lived, occupied the country and enjoyed their pleasure and their possessions. That they lived to some purpose, and how well they accomplished it, a brief comparison of the period of two hundred years ago with the present time will amply prove . . ." (Address by Alfred Paschall to the Bucks County Historical Society on the occasion of the two-hundredth anniversary of the founding of the county, 1882)

Many American celebrations and holidays are religious or traditional rather than patriotic. Christmas, a mixture of pagan and Christian traditions, was not widely celebrated here until the 18th century, and many of the customs and objects that we associate with the holiday—Santa Claus, the Christmas tree, and gift giving—are late-19th-century

Thanksgiving place markers or souvenirs, papier-mâché; United States, 1920–40. These turkeys would have been placed about the table during the Thanksgiving feast. The one at right has a bottom that opens to receive candy. Also found are turkey-form candles and napkins decorated with the providential bird.

Thanksgiving, oil on canvas; by Mattie Lou O'Kelley, Georgia, 1982. The traditional Thanksgiving feast has long been part of American life. O'Kelley's version reflects the warm feelings she retains for her country home and close family ties.

arrivals. Even so, a rich body of folk art and artifacts has already grown up around this holiday.

Among the most charming creations associated with Christmas are the blown-glass decorations that add color to the Christmas tree. There are also Christmas cards, Santa Claus costumes, and even the elaborate painted-wood constructions displayed outside some homes during the holiday season.

Other holidays, such as Easter, Halloween, and the New Orleans Mardi Gras, have inspired American folk artists. Halloween costumes, masks, candle lanterns, and party favors have a charming folk quality. Illustrated here are a toy accordion, a bell and rattles, candy boxes in the shape of witches and goblins, and a large papier-mâché pumpkin probably intended as a table centerpiece.

Mardi Gras has produced some of the most spectacular masks and costumes of the 20th century, and some of these are true works of art, handed down from year to year by those who take part in the traditional parade.

Because the United States is a great "melting pot" of races and nationalities, it is the scene of many diverse ethnic holidays and festivals. Saint Patrick's Day, for example, has become a national holiday, with all races and national groups joining in—and everyone claiming to be Irish. Other important ethnic holidays include the Chinese New Year, celebrated in every city with a large Chinese population, Puerto Rican Independence Day, and various religious festivals. Old customs and celebrations may be dying away in other parts of the world, but in America, the number of traditional ethnic celebrations increases yearly.

Some celebrations occur only periodically. For example, the anniversaries of the founding of various American cities are celebrated at hundred-year intervals. The greatest of these events, the centennial and bicentennial of American independence, inspired the production of vast quantities of folk painting and sculpture.

The events surrounding the centennial of the Statue of Liberty provided yet another subject for folk artists, who created works that range from remarkable folk paintings, such as the example illustrated here by contemporary artist Milton Bond, to an array of wood, metal, and ceramic objects.

These are but a part of the many traditional family, ethnic, and regional holidays that enrich the American scene and have been faithfully recorded, over the years, by folk artists and craftsmen. While the celebrations of some holidays have dwindled or passed away over the years—Arbor Day, almost forgotten today, was once the occasion of great excitement among American schoolchildren—new holidays are emerging as new groups reach our shores, and thus the tradition goes on.

Easter at the White House, mixed media on canvas; by Janet Munro, New York, 1985. Painted at special request for the White House, this charming work captures a new American tradition—the annual egg-rolling and associated festivities sponsored by the president.

ABOVE: Christmas-tree ornaments, blown glass; Germany and the United States, late 19th and early 20th centuries. Though the decorated Christmas tree as we know it did not appear until well into the 1800s, a remarkable variety of hand-blown folk art decorations have since been created. OPPOSITE: *A Gift from the Magi*, acrylic on canvas; by Barbara Bustetter Falk, Tucson, Arizona, 1982. Falk captures the spirit of Christmas while at the same time adding a whimsical touch all her own. The tree's ornaments include symbols of Christ taken from Christian art—the small bird at right, however, represents a falcon and is a symbol for "Falk."

ABOVE: Halloween accordion, lithographed paper, cardboard, tissue paper, and wood; United States, 1900–20. Never intended as a musical instrument, this toy was probably carried by trick or treaters on their nocturnal rounds. RIGHT: Halloween pumpkin, papier-mâché with painted features; United States, 1890–1910. Probably intended as a table centerpiece, this charming pumpkin is a true bit of folk art and a rare survivor from an earlier age. OPPOSITE TOP, LEFT TO RIGHT: Halloween noisemakers; United States, 1920–40. Bell made of lithographed wood and metal. Combination rattle-horn made of wood and cardboard. Rattle made of lithographed tin. OPPOSITE BOTTOM: Halloween candy containers, papier-mâché, straw, cardboard, and paper; United States, 1900–30. The heads of the figures can be removed to insert sweets. Folk art collectors look for examples, such as these, with charming and unusual features.

Halloween Still Life, acrylic on canvas; by Susan Slyman, New York, 1984. There are few paintings related to Halloween, so this charming version is particularly appreciated. Note the interesting detail of the children wending their way on trick or treat.